A BACKYARD PRAIRIE

A
BACKYARD
PRAIRIE

THE
HIDDEN BEAUTY
OF TALLGRASS
AND WILDFLOWERS

Fred Delcomyn and
James L. Ellis

Southern Illinois University Press
Carbondale

Southern Illinois University Press
www.siupress.com

24 23 22 21   4 3 2 1

Photographs by Fred Delcomyn, except where noted

Cover illustration and frontispiece: A tallgrass prairie in summer

Library of Congress Cataloging-in-Publication Data
Names: Delcomyn, Fred, author. | Ellis, James L., [date] author. |
    Berenbaum, M. (May), foreword.
Title: A backyard prairie : the hidden beauty of tallgrass and wildflowers
    / Fred Delcomyn, James L. Ellis, foreword by May Berenbaum.
Description: Carbondale : Southern Illinois University Press, 2021. |
    Includes bibliographical references.
Identifiers: LCCN 2020041498 (print) | LCCN 2020041499 (ebook) |
    ISBN 9780809338184 (paperback) | ISBN 9780809338191 (ebook)
Subjects: LCSH: Prairies. | Prairie ecology.
Classification: LCC QK938.P7 D453 2021 (print) | LCC QK938.P7 (ebook) |
    DDC 577.4/4—dc23
LC record available at https://lccn.loc.gov/2020041498
LC ebook record available at https://lccn.loc.gov/2020041499

Printed on recycled paper ♻

To Christie Henry, Kim Bookless, and Katherine Don, three remarkable women with a passion for books and publishing.

Without their encouragement and enthusiasm for this project, it might never have come to fruition.

CONTENTS

ILLUSTRATIONS

8. OPEN SKY

FINAL IMAGE

FOREWORD

Almost 20 years ago, landscapers at the University of Illinois at Urbana-Champaign (UIUC) experimented with planting prairie grasses at a newly refurbished entryway onto the campus; within days, complaints flooded administrative offices that the grasses looked "weedy" and unkempt and were altogether ill suited to the purpose of impressing campus visitors. The prairie grasses were duly removed and replaced with neatly trimmed lawn and conventional garden flowers. Over the next two decades, however, campus officials, alumni, and students, as well as people in the wider world beyond the campus, have gained a much better understanding of tallgrass prairies and a deeper appreciation for the natural heritage of Illinois and its perilous present state. The reviled "weedy" plants that briefly greeted campus visitors included little bluestem, one of the more conspicuous elements of tallgrass prairie communities. The prairie soil of much of Illinois, Iowa, and neighboring states has the misfortune of being among the world's most fertile and productive for agriculture; what were once trackless acres of bluestem grasses are now for the most part vast acres of corn and soybeans. Today, although Illinois still claims as its nickname the Prairie State, less than 0.01 percent of the original tallgrass prairie that once blanketed the state remains, tiny remnants almost lost amid agricultural fields, towns, and cities.

Just because it's now so easy to overlook the prairies doesn't mean they deserve to be overlooked. In fact, even in their vastly reduced extent, they are wonders of species diversity, dynamic ecological change, and exceptional natural beauty. When retired professor of entomology Fred Delcomyn and his wife, Nancy, bought a house and some land adjoining a cornfield (like so many properties here in central Illinois) just a short distance from the UIUC campus, they were inspired to restore the half of their five acres that had been farmed to a closer approximation of its original state. Undoing a century or more of human disturbance was not a task to be accomplished overnight. Bringing back the prairie to the Prairie State, even on a small scale, requires hard work, meticulous planning, relentless attention to detail, and above all, patience. Finding an experienced partner is an enormous help, and Fred was fortunate to find James Ellis, a botanist with the Prairie Research Institute at UIUC who was the president of a local conservation group dedicated to preserving and restoring natural landscapes, including tallgrass prairie, to east-central Illinois. Jamie's experience was essential to the restoration effort.

Prairies are finicky, as plant communities go—they need periodic burning to maintain their identity. But managed burns must be done with care, not only because of the risk they present to people and property but also, ironically, because of the risk they present to the flora and fauna that the prairie comprises. If they're too hot or too wide-ranging, the less mobile inhabitants will be imperiled. Growing corn is challenging, even here in central Illinois, but growing a prairie is infinitely more complicated.

Fortunately for readers, not only does Fred have patience, but he also has an entomologist's view of the world. Noticing and appreciating little things are a career requirement and professional obligation for entomologists. He also has mad skills as a photographer, and he has succeeded in capturing many captivating moments in the recovery of this gorgeous little prairie. It's our good fortune that he is willing, through this book, to share those moments with us. A black-and-gold bumble bee feeding on a white wild indigo flower, a song sparrow perched on a thistle, paw prints of a coyote in the snow—these are just a few of the dozens of amazing, indelible images of life in a tallgrass prairie that Fred has noticed, captured, preserved, and shared.

Affection for the prairie and its denizens here in the Midwest is everywhere apparent—in the engaging and informative text and the artful and revelatory photographs. As this book documents the restoration (or rescue?) of a small piece of a profoundly altered landscape to an approximation of a state more natural and appropriate for this part of the world, it offers lessons not only for neighbors nearby, including those at the land grant university that has now learned to appreciate what it has in the Prairie State, but also for readers everywhere who have a passion for natural and cultural history and a regard for preserving our biological heritage.

May Berenbaum, Department of Entomology, University of Illinois
July 2021

A BACKYARD PRAIRIE

INTRODUCTION

It's safe to say that the foundations of the backyard prairie, this book, and the friendship of the coauthors were laid in the year 2001. Fred Delcomyn and Jamie Ellis did not know each other then, but that year Fred and his wife, Nancy, bought a five-acre tract of land just south of Urbana, Illinois. Half the tract was wooded, mainly black walnut and hackberry, with a house nestled among the trees; the other half was being farmed.

The transformation of the farmed half to prairie was accomplished over the space of two years. Visitors to the backyard prairie occasionally ask how it came to be. After all, most people, when buying five rural acres, do not immediately think, "Let's plant a prairie!" Fred and Nancy, though, being avid outdoors people, thought that it would be interesting if the half being farmed were restored to a landscape resembling the prairie that once covered more than half the state of Illinois. Since they love natural places and were well acquainted with the long history of prairie in east-central Illinois, it was an obvious step to think that planting something resembling the tallgrass prairie that had covered the land 200 years ago might be both interesting and visually appealing. As it was, walking out the front door and seeing soybeans or corn just beyond the flower garden was not very attractive, and the income from farming was minimal.

In 2003, after some research and with help from the Illinois Department of Natural Resources and its Acres for Wildlife program, the farmed area was seeded with prairie grasses and wildflowers. The adventure had begun.

A critical element in historical prairie was fire. That's where Jamie came into the picture. Fred and Nancy knew that their new prairie should be burned periodically. Some investigation soon identified Grand Prairie Friends, a local conservation group, as an organization that could not only

An aerial view of the backyard prairie in September 2003, the year the prairie was first seeded, shows walking paths. Photo © American Images; used by permission.

1

provide advice but also help in managing prescribed burns. Jamie was a little taken aback by Fred's initial email, which we can paraphrase as "Your website is outdated; are you still a viable organization?" It was not quite that brusque (Fred is usually more polite), but that was the message Jamie remembers. At the time, Jamie was the president of Grand Prairie Friends, and he enthusiastically agreed to help manage the new prairie. His day job, as a botanist with the University of Illinois's Prairie Research Institute, gave him a unique perspective on prairie plants and what it takes to keep them healthy.

Volunteers from Grand Prairie Friends conducted the first burn of the entire prairie in late February 2005, two years after the initial seeding. It was a complete success, although at one point Fred and Nancy were a bit unnerved to see smoke and flame nearly obscuring the nearby house. Grand Prairie Friends, an organization the couple quickly joined, has burned a portion of the prairie every year since then, keeping the prairie ecosystem in good health. The annual burns also provide a wonderful spectacle that many friends have found awe-inspiring.

To understand the origins of this book, fast-forward to 2010. Fred and Nancy periodically showed their flourishing prairie to visitors—not only people affiliated with Grand Prairie Friends but also others who had no special interest in prairie. Reactions ranged from great surprise that such a beautiful prairie could exist near a city to wondrous appreciation of a reconstructed natural area. The keen interest of both friends and prairie experts prompted Fred and Jamie to write an article on the prairie for a local magazine. The article was a great success and led to the idea that many more people could gain an appreciation of small prairie if we were to write a whole book about it.

There are other books on prairie. However, these typically concentrate on prairies that encompass hundreds or thousands of acres. Consequently, the books inevitably leave the impression that only very large projects are being undertaken and that only those large projects can lead to an appreciation of the enormous expanse of prairie that once covered most of central North America.

Our experience with this 2.5-acre re-created prairie, and with small remnants of original prairie in east-central Illinois and elsewhere, leads to a rather different conclusion. The beauty of nature is everywhere—you just have to know where to look for it and how to appreciate it.

The goal of our book is simple: to show the beauty found in a small

prairie. We meet this purpose through photographs and text. Most of the photographs were taken in or near the backyard prairie, and the text flows from the experience of observing this prairie for more than a decade and a half.

We hope that by looking through our eyes and reading our words you will also appreciate this beauty and will be inspired to visit and take a closer look at the small remnants of prairie that can be found throughout Illinois and its neighboring states where the tallgrass prairie once thrived. If you do, this book will have more than fulfilled its purpose.

A panoramic view of the prairie in early summer shows the walking path that wends through it. The tree at the far right is a bur oak, a prominent feature of savannas in the prairie, since its thick bark allows it to withstand fire.

CHAPTER 1

GLIMPSES OF THE PAST,
REALITY OF THE PRESENT

*The Illinois country is undeniably the most beautiful that is known
anywhere between the mouth of the St. Lawrence River and that of
the Mississippi, which are a thousand leagues apart.*
—Sieur Pierre Deliette, 1695

As I look west from my backyard prairie across the rolling landscape of
central Illinois, I try to imagine what it would have been like standing here 20,000 years ago. What would I have seen? Certainly not prairie.
No verdant fields of flowers. No animals either. Just ice, miles and miles
of unbroken glacier, perhaps hundreds of feet thick. Yet merely 250 years
ago on the same spot, I would have seen an expanse of prairie many miles
wide, nearly unbroken by any trees. Grasses and wildflowers carpeted the
landscape, the very definition of prairie.

How did the vast expanse of tallgrass prairie come to be? Two factors
were critical: climate and fire. First, climate played a significant role by
allowing the formation of enormous glaciers over the northern part of central North America. Second, a dry and warm period favored prairie over
forest, which, combined with fire, further pushed the formation of prairie.

Continent-wide glaciers formed and then melted multiple times over a
period of 1.5 million years. They scoured the earth over which they flowed,
crushing all plant life and leveling the landscape.

The most recent glaciation, called the Wisconsinan, was at its peak
around 20,000 years ago. You might think that as climate warmed in the
ensuing years, the glaciers covering the area would simply have melted
away, allowing the prairie to grow in its place. Geological and paleoecolog-
ical evidence suggests it was nowhere near this simple.

*A typical view in the region: what was
once covered by tallgrass prairie is now
farm fields and human development.*

Instead, there was a long, complex dance between the advancing or retreating front of the glacier and the forest—not prairie—that usually occupied the exposed land beyond the glacier's edge. Over thousands of years, the edge of the glacier advanced, stalled, retreated, and then advanced again, until finally retreating for good. This process produced moraines, long ridges of rock, debris, and sediment deposited where the glacier stopped advancing. Many moraines have elevations of 50 feet and more above the surrounding land, and they crisscross east-central Illinois and other glaciated regions. Fifty feet may not seem like much, but on an otherwise flat landscape, it was enough to have a significant impact on water flow, creating dry areas on the ridgetops and marshy areas here and there throughout.

Now I imagine myself 5,000 to 10,000 years later than the glacier-dominated scene I first envisioned. The glacier has finally melted and receded for good, leaving at first a barren and mostly flat terrain, covered by a layer of ground-up soil and crushed rock, in many places hundreds of feet thick. Over hundreds of years, the newly exposed land will be invaded by plants well adapted to grow on soil with few nutrients and no organic matter, and eventually by trees forming a fir and spruce forest of the type now seen in northern Canada. Such trees were and are well adapted to grow in what was, after all, still a cold climate.

A country road undulates its way up and over a moraine. This moraine formed about 10,000 years ago during the last ice age, when a glacier stalled, neither advancing nor retreating, and deposited its load of rocky debris at the end or sides. Stalling occurred when the front of a glacier melted as fast as the pressure of ice from the north kept it moving forward. Geographic features of the modern landscape such as moraines are evidence of events of previous epochs.

Hardwood forests like this one once covered much of the tallgrass region, a few thousand years after the last glacier had retreated 10,000 to 12,000 years ago. Oak and hickory were the dominant trees.

As the climate warmed and the glacier retreated farther north, the fir and spruce were replaced by hardwood trees like hickory and oak, better adapted to the warmer environmental conditions.

This hardwood forest is what I likely would have seen 10,000 years ago. But then, where did the prairie come from? Here another climatic change was crucial, a warm and dry period (indicated in the fossil record by a change from trees that need plenty of water to plants that are more tolerant of drier conditions) that began perhaps 9,000 years ago and lasted for about 4,000 years. This dry period limited growth or killed most kinds of trees that had grown in the area and allowed the invasion of drought-tolerant prairie plants.

One trait that made prairie plants so successful is also the trait that later delayed exploitation of the prairie for growing crops—an incredibly

7

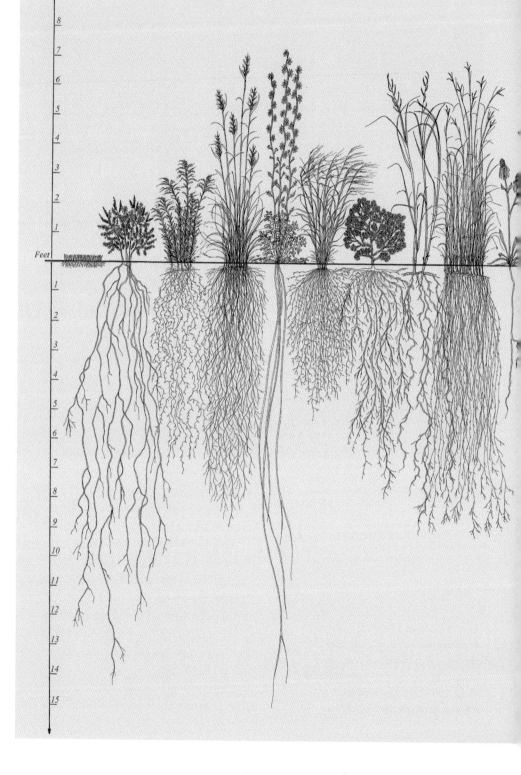

This drawing graphically illustrates one of the secrets to the prairie's success—the plants' astonishing root systems. The roots of many prairie plants extend down as far as the plant soars above the ground, 10 to 12 feet in some cases. Deep roots help prairie plants survive drought, grazing, and fire. Drawing by Heidi Natura © 1995; used by permission of Heidi Natura and Living Habitats.

8

deep, complex, and extensive root system. Many prairie plants have roots that extend far down into the soil, sometimes deeper than the plant is high. Some plants easily reach a height of 8 to 10 feet; this means that their roots may extend this far as well. For many decades, it was thought that prairie plants drew water through these deep roots. Recent studies, however, suggest it's not that simple.

Prairie grasses have most of their root mass in a fine, dense tangle in the top foot or so of the soil. They have deeper roots as well, but it appears that they draw water mainly through this upper layer of roots. Prairie wildflowers, on the other hand, seem to draw water from roots down to about 2.5 feet. They also have much deeper roots, but the role of these deep roots remains a mystery. In contrast, turf grasses and many garden plants have shallow root systems; the roots of some grasses extend only a few inches into the soil, and the roots of some garden flowers extend only a foot. Prairie stays green even after months without rain, while your garden and lawn will become depressingly dry and drab without supplemental water.

The vibrant green of prairie plant leaves persists well into the hot and often dry summer months, a beautiful backdrop for the diverse and colorful mid-July array of flowers. This image shows wild bergamot (violet flowers), Culver's root (spears of white flower at far left), gray-headed coneflower (yellow flowers with dark centers, left), and false sunflower (cuplike yellow flowers).

A prairie fire burns in late winter. In precolonial times, when prairie covered the landscape of central Illinois, fires like this maintained prairie over forest vegetation by killing tree seedlings. Deep-rooted prairie plants thrive after fire.

It is likely that 9,000 years ago, there were few humans around to witness this change from wet to dry conditions. Certainly, no evidence of humans has been found in east-central Illinois that dates back that far.

But by the time the climate once again became wet enough to sustain the growth of forests, Native Peoples had established themselves in the area and had begun to introduce the second factor critical to the establishment of the prairie seen by the early explorers—fire.

Ecologists in the early twentieth century recognized that periodic fire kills most trees before they are large enough to survive a fire. This fact was crucial to the maintenance of the tallgrass prairie. Without fire, the tallgrass prairie extending from Minnesota down through Iowa and Illinois to Missouri would have been overgrown by the eastern hardwood forests, which covered much of what became Ohio and Indiana to the east.

Fires could start naturally in prairie, ignited by lightning strikes. This likely happened occasionally in the late fall and early spring, when active growth had retreated underground and the dead stems of prairie plants were not wet from rain or covered in snow. Such intermittent fires may

11

by themselves have been enough to suppress tree growth on the prairie, but humans also intervened. As reported by early explorers and settlers, Native Peoples deliberately set fire to the prairie in order to drive game (making it easier to hunt), to improve game habitat (making it more attractive to grazers like bison), and to keep trees out (making it easier to see game from a distance). In recent years, ecologists have come to the conclusion that this human intervention was crucial in keeping the eastern forests at bay.

The combined forces of climate and fire helped establish and then maintain the tallgrass prairie. Tallgrass prairie covered most of Iowa and Illinois, extending into Minnesota and Missouri to the north and south, as well as westward into parts of Nebraska, the Dakotas, and other states. Farther west, the rain shadow cast by the Rocky Mountains prevented the growth of most trees even without fire. The composition of this shortgrass prairie was a bit different as well, consisting of shorter grasses and more drought-tolerant wildflowers.

Fast forward to 250 years ago. If I had been able to stand at the site of the backyard prairie in the late eighteenth century, I would have seen a vast, open, apparently featureless space stretching nearly to the horizon as far as the eye could see—an area named the Grand Prairie by early explorers and settlers. Altogether, it is estimated that about 60 percent (about 22 million acres) of Illinois was prairie when the first Europeans appeared on the scene.

Featureless perhaps to explorer and settler eyes used to nothing but forest to the north and the east, the prairie was not at all lacking in biological diversity. There was grass, certainly. Some kinds, like Indian grass and big bluestem, were as tall as eight feet. But the prairie was so much more, with different combinations of grasses and wildflowers prospering in different places, depending on the type and wetness of the soil. Furthermore, tallgrass prairie contained a profusion of wildflowers, many hundreds of species, so that from May to October, different kinds of plants added a riot of color to what otherwise seemed to be a monotonous landscape.

As noted by Judge James Hall in 1838:

> The scenery of the prairie is striking and never fails to cause an exclamation of surprise. . . . The verdure and the flowers are beautiful; the absence of shade, and consequent appearances of profusion of light, produce a gaiety which animates the beholder.

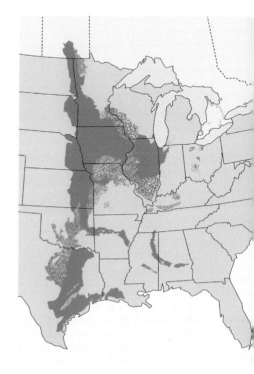

A map of the Midwestern United States shows the approximate range of tallgrass prairie before European settlement, before the land was converted to agricultural uses. Experts disagree as to the exact location of the eastern and western boundaries of the tallgrass region. Sparse historical records and the fluid nature of the prairie and forest boundary due to weather and fire conditions make determination of the boundaries difficult. Copyright © by Daryl Smith and Brent Butler, Tallgrass Prairie Center; used by permission.

Grasses grow tall at Prospect Cemetery Prairie Nature Preserve in Illinois, a small, protected remnant of the original prairie. The defining plants of the tallgrass prairie are tall grasses, such as Indian grass, big bluestem, and switchgrass, which could reach eight feet in height when conditions were favorable.

The early explorers hardly knew what to make of the vast expanse of prairie. The word *prairie* itself comes from the French and means "meadow." But French explorers had little to compare to the North American prairie, since Europe was mostly forested or in agriculture in the sixteenth and seventeenth centuries. As a consequence, Europeans thought the prairie, with its decided lack of trees, was infertile and no place to settle. What they did not realize at first was that the soil of the prairie, having been built up by thousands of years of profuse plant growth, was some of the most fertile in the world.

Tragically, Native Peoples were forced out of Illinois, and eventually, the prairie was settled, mostly in the nineteenth century, by descendants of those who originally came from Europe. At first settlements were confined

This prairie restoration in a forest preserve in Illinois gives a hint of the profusion of color noted by early travelers. A view in early August shows wild bergamot (the violet flowers), cup plant (the tallest, yellow-flowered plants), gray-headed coneflower (plants with gray immature seed heads surrounded by yellow petals), and a smattering of purple coneflower (the small reddish-purple flowers).

A profile of soil shows what developed under tallgrass prairie. These soils, known as mollisols, are dark because of their highly organic content, which extends far down below the surface. The scale in this photograph is in centimeters, so this profile is about 19 inches deep. Mollisols are nutrient-rich and generally support productive agriculture. Photo courtesy of USDA Natural Resources Conservation Service, Illinois.

to groves of trees that were scattered throughout the prairie in areas with some protection from fire. These groves were dominated by bur oak, a tree with exceptionally thick bark that allows it to withstand fire. Where conditions were right, often centered on the natural protected valley formed by a stream and the surrounding wet area, these groves dotted the landscape.

Early settlers, looking for shelter and resources with which to build houses, wagons, and plows, congregated in these areas. It wasn't long until they realized that the prairie, far from being barren, actually had astonishing fertility. Over the 9,000 or so years since the prairie first formed, the cycle of growth and decay had resulted in a rich and fertile soil laden with organic matter and many feet thick.

Exploitation of the prairie did not come quickly or easily, however. In the East, farmers had their share of challenges in establishing working farms, as they had to clear the land of trees and brush and remove the rocks that were strewn all over the landscape.

On the prairie, the challenges were entirely different. The lack of trees was a decided advantage, certainly. Further, except for the occasional glacial erratic, large or even huge boulders left by the retreating glaciers, the landscape was devoid of rocks to clear.

Instead, the challenge was in the soil itself. The heavy black prairie earth, laced throughout with a thick tangle of roots, proved exceptionally

15

challenging to work with the wood and iron plows available at the beginning of the nineteenth century. It has been reported that three men and a team of four oxen could break only about an acre of prairie a day. Even after this initial breakup of prairie, it was still slow going. The soil was difficult to work; much of it contained a significant component of clay, making it sticky, and it was filled with strong, fibrous roots. For this reason, the farmer could not simply pull a plow through the soil but was forced to stop frequently to scrape off the accumulated clay-laden soil. This stop-and-go mode of plowing was a major reason that it was such a slow process.

The invention of the self-scouring steel plow by John Deere in 1837 changed everything by allowing that rich soil to be turned more easily, without the frequent stops formerly necessary. The sticky soil slid off the hard, polished steel. The sizes of farms and the productivity of the land

A granite rock, known as a glacial erratic, is surrounded by prairie vegetation. This rock may have been placed in the prairie restoration where it now lies, but rocks this size and larger were deposited throughout the prairie by melting glaciers. Geologists know this occurred because no granite is in the bedrock of this part of Illinois. Photo taken at the Lake Park Prairie Restoration, Savoy, Illinois.

increased enormously as the prairie was plowed under. By the late nineteenth century, the vast expanses of grasses and wildflowers were mostly gone. A. W. Herre, writing in 1940, noted,

> *I returned to the region [Illinois] several summers during the 1890s, but the prairie as such had disappeared, and of course, its characteristic life with it. What a pity that some of it could not have been preserved, so that those born later might enjoy its beauty.*

It is estimated that before 1800, tallgrass prairie occupied roughly half of the combined area of Illinois, Iowa, Minnesota, and Missouri, the four major tallgrass states. In about 70 years, however, from 1830 to 1900, the early settlers and their descendants turned that wonderfully fertile soil into one of the world's most productive agricultural regions. Unfortunately, no one considered conserving any prairie. Today in Illinois, less than 0.01 percent of the original prairie remains, mostly in cemeteries, along abandoned railroad rights-of-way, and on land that can't readily be plowed.

Whereas centuries ago a traveler could see unbroken miles of prairie, today one sees only unbroken miles of row crops such as corn and soybeans. Iowa and Illinois, for example, seem to vie each year for producing the most corn in the United States. About 60 percent of the area of the four tallgrass prairie states is now devoted to farming. The days of the unbroken prairie are indeed long gone.

Rows of soybeans sprout in a central Illinois field shortly after spring planting. Fields of soybeans, along with rows upon rows of corn, are a typical rural scene in the tallgrass prairie states now.

CHAPTER 2

FARMLAND TO PRAIRIE

Perhaps, ironically, the destruction of the prairie by our forebears as they strove for a better life in the new world has led to a level of material comfort which affords us the luxury to consider its preservation for future generations. —Walter Mirk, 1997

Left, equipment is lined up, ready to begin seeding the backyard prairie in June 2003. Above, a headstone dated 1846 is now part of Fairchild Cemetery Savanna Nature Preserve in Vermilion County, Illinois. Remnants of the once vast tallgrass prairie can be found in some pioneer cemeteries, which have been an important source of seeds of native prairie plants.

The silence was nearly complete, broken only by the rustle of leaves as a slight breeze blew though the nearby trees. It was a spring afternoon in a pioneer cemetery, the weathered gravestones testifying to a time long gone when life was hard and often short. As we and our companions walked among the headstones, we saw scattered reminders of another time—descendants of the original prairie flowers and grasses that once covered the landscape. This little bit of original prairie was what we hoped to re-create when we started on the journey to convert a patch of farmland to prairie.

In the nineteenth century, life on the prairie was not easy, and neither settlers nor explorers gave much thought to saving any of the seemingly endless prairie. Keeping body and soul together or seeing what lay beyond the horizon took all their attention.

In more recent decades, however, the necessity of working all day for an uncertain outcome is now behind us, and people have begun to recognize the grandeur of what was lost. The small patches of remnant prairie, in unmowed pioneer cemeteries, here and there along abandoned railroad rights-of-way, or on land too steep, rocky, or sandy to turn into agricultural fields, provide refuges for the plants that once dominated the landscape. From these remnants, seeds were harvested, and the new activity of prairie restoration and reconstruction took hold.

Some of the restorations have involved thousands of acres and millions of dollars. Places like the 3,800-acre Nachusa Grasslands in Illinois and the 8,600-acre Neal Smith National Wildlife Refuge prairie restoration in Iowa, as well as similar restoration efforts in Minnesota and Missouri, are prime examples. Visitors certainly come away from visiting these places awestruck at the vast scale and beauty of open prairie.

Other restorations have been much more modest in scale. Forest preserve districts, state and federal agencies, and nonprofit conservation groups in prairie states are making an effort to restore a few dozen to a few hundred acres to prairie. These efforts show that thousand-acre restorations are not the only way to recreate prairie.

On an even smaller scale, private individuals are re-creating prairie on only a few acres. Our backyard prairie is a prime example of what can be done. However, it is one thing for a well-funded state agency or conservation organization to undertake a prairie restoration, calling on professionals and experts as needed along the way. It's quite another for private individuals with limited funds and no expertise to do the same. So the question does arise: Even if someone has land that could be devoted to prairie, why would that person want to undertake the effort and expense of planting a prairie?

There is no single answer to this question. For us, it can only be said that the thought of being able to enjoy even a small sample of the thousands upon thousands of acres of open prairie that once covered much of Illinois was enticement enough. Although the effort was not trivial, the rewards exceeded our most optimistic hopes.

How did we establish the backyard prairie? Since there was once prairie at our location, you might think that if we simply stopped farming the land, the prairie would spring back from the soil. We realized early on that unfortunately this isn't the case. Plants would certainly grow, just not the ones native to prairie. Nearly two centuries of intensive farming in the Midwest have eliminated virtually all prairie plants from agricultural land, so none is left to reseed an area naturally.

If prairie plants won't spring from the soil spontaneously, that means seeds have to be purchased. Where can you get the seeds? The geographic origin of the seeds has to be matched to the geographic location of the backyard prairie. After all, it won't do much good to purchase seeds from plants growing in western Nebraska if they are to be planted in eastern Illinois. The ecological regions are different enough that plants that thrive in one region are unlikely to thrive in the other.

At the inception of the backyard prairie in June 2003, furrows were created by the equipment used to score the soil gently in preparation for seeding. They are still visible here after the seeds had been spread. The unplowed strip in the center of the photo is the course of a planned walking path running through the prairie.

Fortunately, many companies offer seeds of prairie plants, and most of these companies will make the best match that they can between the seeds they sell you and your location.

As we discovered, however, picking a seed company is actually the easiest part of seed selection. The bigger question is what seeds to buy. It's not unusual to be overwhelmed at this point. A healthy native prairie can easily contain 150 different species of flowering plants and grasses, far too many to consider for individuals with limited resources. How did we choose?

Plant selection for the backyard prairie was fundamentally pragmatic. Rather than spending weeks or months reading about the pros and cons of including (or not) a particular species, we went with two pretty simple criteria: Are the flowers attractive, and when do they appear? With a mix of flowering plants that bloomed from May through September and even into October, we would likely have a prairie that had something to offer throughout the entire growing season. Throw in some legumes like purple prairie clover (to provide nitrogen fixation for the soil), and we were good to go.

Seeding 2.5 acres would have been a challenge. We didn't possess the equipment to do this, and seeding by hand seemed overwhelming. Fortunately, the Illinois Department of Natural Resources had a program called Acres for Wildlife for just this purpose. In exchange for converting land to something closer to its original natural state, the department would provide personnel and equipment to seed the area. We arranged to have the work done in early June.

Once the hard work of planning, preparing, and planting had been done, we hoped that we would be able to sit back and enjoy the fruits of our labors immediately. Not quite! We found that expecting (or at least hoping) to see all our beautiful prairie flowers bloom the first year was unrealistic. It turns out that patience is a virtue—especially when it comes to re-creating prairie, a lesson we learned well.

Two factors worked against a quick result. First, there was an abundance of weed seeds—the ubiquitous, unwanted visitors of the modern agricultural landscape—still in the soil, just waiting to sprout. In fact, during our first year, we were dismayed to see mostly horseweed, velvetleaf, brome, and other unwelcome, fast-growing plants in the space where we were expecting prairie flowers.

Second, most prairie plants are long-lived perennials that send down extremely deep roots. It can take years for this root system to develop enough for the plant to send up flowering shoots. In our prairie, a typical

21

planting in many ways, about half the flowering plants did not bloom for the first several years, and some did not bloom for more than five years.

Nevertheless, in spite of the abundance of weeds and the prairie flowers' need to grow deep roots, the first few years of the backyard prairie showed promising signs of the prairie to come, as the plant population transitioned from agricultural weeds to prairie flowers and grasses. Even in the first year after planting, flowers such as black-eyed Susan and white prairie clover appeared among the ubiquitous horseweed, brome, and other unwanted plants that dominated the site. The second year saw even more prairie flowers, such as rosinweed and gray-headed coneflower, begin to make an appearance.

However, the second year also revealed weed problems that persisted for some time. Most of the unwanted weeds were not able to compete successfully with the native prairie flowers and grasses. They disappeared over time. There were two exceptions to this general rule: giant ragweed and Canada thistle.

Giant ragweed is a native annual plant that thrives in moist, disturbed soil. It is ubiquitous in the tallgrass states. Unfortunately, it was able to thrive in our prairie as well, and after a few years, we had a dense stand in the moist land at the south end of our prairie. In the end, physical removal by uprooting or cutting the plants was the only effective control. The

22

Above left, the first year after seeding of the backyard prairie produced the yellow flowers of black-eyed Susan, one of the early bloomers in prairie reconstructions. But the predominant plant is the tall, slender horseweed, visible in this photo. Horseweed is a native weedy annual that readily grows in disturbed soils across the prairie region but does not persist once prairie plants have become established. Above, white prairie clover is in the bean, or legume, family. Not as conspicuous as black-eyed Susan, it is another early bloomer in prairie reconstructions. This photo was taken in June of the first year after seeding the backyard prairie. We included this species for its bright white flowers and its ability to fix nitrogen, a vital but limited soil nutrient.

infestation is now minimal, but removal of the stray plants that take root in the prairie is necessary every year to prevent a recurrence.

Canada thistle was an even more severe problem. This perennial weed is an aggressive invasive that spreads by rhizomes (horizontal roots) underground, as well as by seed. Once a stand of Canada thistle was established in our prairie, only persistent mechanical removal along with herbicides worked to control it. Fortunately, herbicide could be used because the plant greens up in the spring weeks before the native prairie plants. That helps it get a leg up on growth for the year; it also makes it susceptible to applications of herbicide, which do not hurt the native species because they don't yet have any aboveground growth.

Dealing with weeds and waiting for our prairie to grow was at times frustrating, indeed. But the thrill of seeing a new flower in the prairie for the first time after many years of waiting is beyond description. Once established, our prairie has given us a summerlong show of brilliant colors that is there rain or shine, drought or deluge. A neighbor's yard and garden might wilt or drown, but our bit of re-created prairie has flourished.

Above, *gray-headed coneflower, a June bloomer, made an appearance the second year after planting. Unlike this one, most prairie plants put down deep roots during the first few years rather than expend energy on flowers.* Right, *a stand of giant ragweed makes an appearance in the backyard prairie. With stems eight feet or more tall, the reason for its name is obvious. This native annual species does well in disturbed soil, particularly in areas that flood. With time, it will usually fade away as other plants become established. It can, however, take over a prairie if not managed.*

CHAPTER 3

FIRE

*I had often heard of the grand spectacle they present when on fire,
and was fortunate enough to witness it. . . . [T]he flames . . .
appeared actually to leap forward and dart into the grass, several
yards in advance of the line. It passed me like a whirlwind, and
with a fury I shall never forget.* —William Blane, 1824

On a warm, sunny day in late March a few years after we had first established our prairie, I stood with a small crew at the ready. We planned to set part of the backyard prairie on fire. The brown, dry stems and leaves, remnants of the previous summer's lush growth, would provide the fuel needed to carry a fire.

Fire! The very word evokes awe and fear. People often view fire—particularly wildfire—as something destructive and to be suppressed. It certainly is a force that can destroy, yet in a prairie, life always returns after the flames have died away. In fact, for thousands of years, fires regularly swept through the prairies. It is likely that the tallgrass prairie could not have existed without fire. Started naturally by lightning or on purpose by Native Peoples, fire played a critical role in maintaining prairie by killing trees and tree seedlings and returning to the soil nutrients bound up in the dead stems and leaves of prairie vegetation.

Historically, prairie fires could occur at any time during the year, but fuel conditions and weather patterns led to fall being the most likely time for a natural or human-set fire to start, with late spring not far behind. Many early nineteenth-century travelers wrote that the Native Peoples would set fire to the prairie every autumn or winter to aid in hunting

A prescribed prairie burn.

25

game, such as bison, deer, elk, and other animals. We chose to burn the backyard prairie in the spring.

Although we could have done so, we were not going to burn the entire 2.5 acres of our prairie; we would burn only about a third of it this year. Portions of the prairie would be left unburned to serve as a refuge for small mammals, such as mice and voles, and the many insects overwintering in the dead stems of prairie plants, animals that otherwise would be killed by the fire. When prairie covered thousands of acres and fire swept across the landscape, there were always small pockets of prairie here and there that did not burn, so it was possible for a burned section to be repopulated by small mammals and insects from these unburned patches.

Most of the work of burning a prairie is done well before we light the first match. Fire is a necessary but dangerous tool, so we made a plan and prepared the site to keep the fire where we wanted it to go and keep it out of where we didn't want it to go. Weather conditions can be unpredictable and greatly influence fire behavior. Add the interaction of wind, moisture, fuels, and topography, and it can be hard to gauge the spread of fire through a prairie precisely.

As we planned for this burn, we took advantage of firebreaks created by the six-foot-wide crushed-rock or mowed-grass walking paths through the prairie. The double-loop path naturally divides the prairie into three sections. Burning only a third of the prairie each year not only helps the health of the prairie but also makes the burns easier to manage.

Firebreaks—areas too wet to burn or without fuel to carry fire—were essential to early settlers as well to protect their homesteads from fire. They could also be important to those travelers unlucky enough to be caught out on an open prairie in the presence of a fire. Travelers' reports from the early nineteenth century advised later visitors that they should always carry materials for starting a fire. Although it appears from these reports that few people were actually caught and killed in a prairie fire, the danger was real enough. If a fire were moving quickly, fanned by the ever-present wind, the only safe way to survive if they could not outrun it was to set their own fire, wait for it to move on, then walk into the freshly burned area. This would serve as a firebreak, and people could wait out the approaching larger fire there in relative safety.

The wind was in the right direction, according to our plan, blowing steadily and just enough to rustle the leaves, but not too strongly. The humidity was also just right, the air being not too dry and not too moist. Our small crew of four people knew the plan, and they were at the ready with

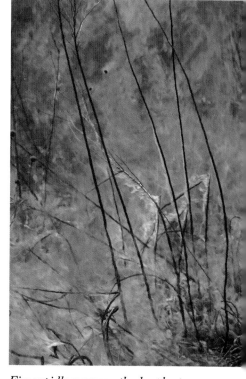

Fire rapidly consumes the dry plant stems of last season's growth. Once started, a prairie fire can be difficult to contain. Prescribed burns are managed by careful preparation, planning for weather conditions and using firebreaks, proper tools, and trained personnel. When prairie covered the landscape, control was impossible, so Native Peoples, settlers, and early visitors had to be prepared to flee the conflagration.

equipment in hand. With all attention on the impending fire, the crew leader struck a match and held it to a dry clump of grass. Almost immediately after the first flames began to feed on the dead plant material, we could feel the heat on our faces and hear the cracking and popping sounds as last year's growth was steadily consumed by the growing fire.

The most important tools at a prairie burn are knowledge and experience. Our crew had been trained and had many years of experience and dozens of fires under their belts. A few hand tools are also invaluable, such as rakes to help move flammable materials out of firebreaks and flappers, broad pieces of rubber attached to wooden handles, to help smother small flames that may start in unwanted places. Backpack water pumpers can quickly douse hot flames. Two-way radios allowed our crew members to communicate conditions from one place in the prairie to another and to coordinate actions to be taken. The right clothes also lessened our crew's risk of harm. They were dressed for the activity with sturdy shoes, leather gloves, fire-resistant suits, helmets, and goggles. To help place the fire where it was wanted, crew members used a drip torch, a small, hand-held tank containing a mix of diesel fuel and gasoline with a spout to dispense the flammable liquid. The drip torch allowed the crew leader to quickly and accurately ignite the prairie.

A member of the burn crew uses a drip torch to ignite a section of the prairie. The drip torch contains a flammable mix of gasoline and diesel fuel. A small flame at the tip acts like a pilot light. When fuel is released, it is ignited and in turn ignites the dead tops of last year's growth of prairie plants. The crushed stone walking path makes a good firebreak.

How does prairie persist and thrive with fire? As we watched the prairie burn, the fire scorched everything, seeming to leave nothing living behind. However, most prairie grasses and wildflowers are perennials. The aboveground stems and leaves die back with the coming of winter and then regrow from deep roots each spring. Growing points are underground, protected from fire. Most fires, driven by the wind, move rapidly across the landscape; soil insulates plant roots from the intense but temporary heat of the fire, which can boil the life out of a green plant.

In contrast, most trees and shrubs have growing points on the stems aboveground. Fires either kill these plants outright or reduce their ability to grow and compete with prairie plants. Some prairie trees and shrubs, such as oaks, sumacs, hazels, and dogwoods, readily resprout from their roots after fire or, once they grow older, develop a thick, corky bark, like that of

Bur oaks are one of the few trees adapted to survive fire. If a seedling is top-killed by fire, it readily resprouts from the roots. Further, the bark of mature trees, which is especially thick, withstands the heat of a fire. Even a young tree like this one (not yet 40 years old) can survive, and indeed it has survived several cycles of fire since it was first planted in the backyard prairie.

28

A head fire (a fire spreading with the wind) roars through the backyard prairie. Flames in these conditions can reach well over a person's head, and the crew must keep careful watch on the fire. The rule of thumb for prescribed burns is that flames can reach two and a half times the height of the tallest vegetation. The crew must use caution and determine that conditions are right before setting a head fire.

a bur oak, which protects them from the heat of the flames. These woody species help form savannas, isolated patches of widely spaced trees and shrubs interspersed among the grasses and wildflowers of the open prairie.

As the fire in the backyard prairie spread, I watched carefully. We had started the fire at the downwind edge up against a gravel path. This backfire consumes fuel into the wind. The flames lean away from dry vegetation, so it burns slowly with little smoke and only one- to two-foot flames. As the fire grew, we worked our way along the downwind edge, creating a blackline—a burned area that won't burn again today. Slowly, the crew set fire to the sides of the prairie, and the fire crackled with more life.

Wind is needed to push the fire, but too much wind might put the fire where it's not wanted. A steady wind is most desired. If wind direction changes after the fire has been started, a slow backfire can turn into an uncontrollable head fire in an instant. This almost happened once in the backyard prairie, and tensions ran high for a while until the wind switched again. When the humidity is high, the dead, fine leaves of prairie grasses soak in moisture, and the fire burns slow and smoky. If the humidity is too low, the prairie can burn hot, fast, and unpredictably.

Eventually, the crew set fire to the prairie on the upwind edge, and it really roared to life. With wind pushing fire into the dry prairie vegetation, flames licked eight feet high or more and moved quickly. A thick plume of white and gray smoke billowed high into the sky. The heat was quite

29

With a sudden shift in the wind and conditions wetter than were thought, smoke from a prairie fire billows up and obscures the owner's house. Burn crews must assess how smoke might affect nearby roads and residential areas. It is important to notify local authorities of a proposed burn so fire trucks don't suddenly show up at your prairie when they're not needed.

intense. At this point, we couldn't have stopped this fire even if we had wanted to with our meager tools. We counted on the success of our plans to limit the fire. When the conflagration reached the blackline and the fuel was entirely consumed, the fire went out almost as quickly as it had started. Within an hour of lighting the match, the fire was done.

Fire generally benefits prairie plants. Grasses such as big bluestem, little bluestem, and Indian grass, which flower late in the summer, grow vigorously after a spring fire. Many wildflowers, such as pale purple coneflower, rattlesnake master, and prairie dock, also seem to flourish the season following a burn. Accumulated plant litter—dead stems and leaves—are consumed, leaving a layer of ash and almost bare soil. The blackened soil exposed to full sunlight warms quickly during lengthening spring days, ensuring regrowth of plants and stimulating seeds to sprout. Research has even shown that smoke promotes the germination of some species, such as pale purple coneflower, stiff goldenrod, and wild quinine. Important nutrients, such as nitrogen and potassium, are returned to the soil in the ash. Small plants and seedlings that might not do well with a thick layer of leaf litter over them are able to grow vigorously after a burn, fostering a rich diversity of plants and a healthy ecosystem.

Humans continue to be—and must be—important managers of remnant and reconstructed prairies. Even in small patches such as the back-yard prairie, periodic fire is an important tool to control unwanted trees

The owner's house can be seen through the flames and heat of a prescribed fire at the backyard prairie. From this angle, the house might seem to be in peril, but there is little danger with a well-executed plan, good control lines and firebreaks, and an experienced crew, all of which were in place in this case.

and shrubs and to stimulate plant growth. It also helps control non-native weeds that are not well adapted to fire. Fire provides all the benefits mentioned above, but it should be treated with respect.

When much of the Illinois landscape was covered with prairie long ago, fires went where they would and stopped when the fuel was consumed, weather conditions changed, or flames met areas too wet to burn. Now we are careful to plan and prepare for fire. We have to be—our house sits only a few dozen feet away from the backyard prairie, and the last thing we want to do is burn it down!

On this day, once the fire had burned itself out, we were left with a pitch-black surface, gray ash scattered here and there, apparently devoid of all life except for a few upright stems that had not burned. Early visitors to the prairie often remarked on the utter desolation left after a fire had swept over thousands of acres of prairie. As one traveler, William Blane, noted in 1824,

> I was always forcibly struck by the melancholy appearance of a burnt Prairie. As far as the eye could reach, nothing was to be seen but one uniform black surface, looking like a vast plain of charcoal. Here and there, by the road side, were the bones of some horses or cattle, which had died in passing through, or the horns of some deer which had been killed.

It was indeed hard to believe that anything would grow in this place again.

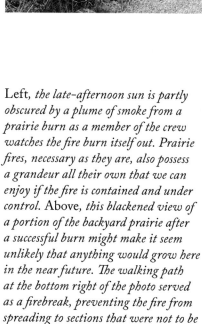

Left, *the late-afternoon sun is partly obscured by a plume of smoke from a prairie burn as a member of the crew watches the fire burn itself out. Prairie fires, necessary as they are, also possess a grandeur all their own that we can enjoy if the fire is contained and under control.* Above, *this blackened view of a portion of the backyard prairie after a successful burn might make it seem unlikely that anything would grow here in the near future. The walking path at the bottom right of the photo served as a firebreak, preventing the fire from spreading to sections that were not to be burned this year.*

Yet each year after we burned part of the backyard prairie, we noticed green shoots poking above the blackened ground a few weeks after the burn. Timing of the burn is also important. If the fire had occurred in late winter as it sometimes did naturally, or early spring, which is when we normally burned, everything would come up fresh and green. If it had been delayed to late spring, when some plants had begun to send up new leaves, we might see new growth with blackened and singed leaf tips.

As the weather warmed and spring made its welcome appearance, we could see another aesthetic benefit to a late-winter burn—it cleared away old growth so that some of the early, low-growing prairie plants could be seen and enjoyed more easily. It seemed that life was always rejuvenated after a fire.

Above right, *a late-spring fire singed the tips of these growing prairie plants. But soil provides good insulation against the quick, intense heat of the fire, so the dense tangle of deep roots was unaffected. Prairie plants will grow new leaves vigorously after a fire.* Right, *shooting stars like this one are spring bloomers— usually in early May in central Illinois. This spectacular flower is rather short and can be hidden by or inconspicuous among the dead thatch of the previous season's growth. Fire clears the prairie so that plants like shooting stars become highly visible.*

33

CHAPTER 4

A RAINBOW LANDSCAPE

You will scarcely credit the profusion of flowers upon these prairies.
We passed whole acres of blossoms all bearing one hue, as purple,
perhaps, or masses of yellow or rose; and then again a carpet of
every color intermixed, or narrow bands, as if a rainbow had fallen
upon the verdant slopes. —Eliza Steele, 1841

It was a typical July day—hot, sunny, humid—when I really noticed it. The prairie had been growing well for five years, but that summer I saw a truly astonishing abundance of compass plants. The plants, their eight-foot-tall stalks festooned with yellow flowers and characteristic deeply incised leaves, were scattered in profusion all over the north section of the prairie. Compass plants had made an appearance in the first few years after the prairie was planted, but I had seen nothing like this before.

It was certainly a joy to see the flowers we had seeded, like compass plant, make an appearance as the years passed. But the prairie brought wonders far beyond simple appearance. This sudden overabundance of a single flower was one of them. It wasn't just compass plants that exhibited a feast-or-famine pattern of growth either. Ohio spiderwort was another species that occasionally showed the same pattern. It was common enough each year, but in some years, spiderwort appeared in such profusion that its deep-blue to purple flowers completely dominated the early-summer prairie.

The sudden surges of flower numbers were not the only fascinating feature of our prairie. Prairie flowers seemed to provide innumerable lessons in ecology for the observant observer, even if the observer is not a specialist in ecology. To stick for the time being to the theme of variability in numbers of flowers, we can mention two others in particular.

Vibrant color is displayed in the prairie throughout the summer and into fall, as shown in this July photo.

35

Compass plants (the tall plants with yellow flowers on the right) may proliferate one year and be inconspicuous the next because of a variety of influences, including rainfall, fire the previous spring, and the average temperature of the winter and spring. The yellow-flowered plants on the left are rosinweed, a close relative of compass plant.

Top, *Ohio spiderwort provides beauty to the prairie in June. This species often shows the same pattern of extraordinary abundance in some years as compass plant. In the case of spiderwort, the main contributing factor seems to be fire, which apparently invigorates these plants. Above, gray-headed coneflowers such as these bloomed the first year after the backyard prairie was planted, and by the eighth year, they were abundant everywhere. After a few more years, however, they were much less common in the interior of the prairie and instead clung mostly to the edges of the paths.*

Black-eyed Susans and gray-headed coneflowers were among the first of the prairie plants to bloom. In fact, both bloomed in significant numbers even the first year after the prairie was seeded. The latter especially seemed to flourish, to such an extent that by the eighth year, gray-headed coneflowers completely dominated parts of the prairie in early summer.

However, by the time another five years had passed, the coneflowers, although still common, no longer dominated the prairie as they once had. Instead, they seemed to cling to the edges of the path that wound its way through the prairie and were less common in the interior.

It seems likely that competition from other plants was the main driving force for the change in the distribution of these coneflowers, although that does not appear to be the case for all plants. Two that were in the initial seed mix, prairie blazing star and rough blazing star, could be seen sparsely scattered about by the third or fourth year after the prairie was established. Over the years, even these few have diminished in number, until by the fifteenth year after the beginning, only one or two plants could be found. In this case, it may have been that the decline of the population was not so much due to competition from other plants as it was to one of the prairie's animal denizens—voles. These small rodents, of which we have plenty in the backyard prairie, are known to feed on the corms (underground, swollen stems somewhat similar to a bulb or tuber) of blazing star plants. We surmise that the voles are at least in part responsible for the demise of the blazing stars.

Other plant populations have gone in the opposite direction. Rattlesnake master, for example, appeared early on but required several more years before it flowered. Once it did, however, it seemed to thrive in the conditions of the backyard prairie, especially the drier north section. And it does especially well the season after prescribed fire. By the tenth year and beyond, the prairie usually showed quite a number of rattlesnake master flowers in midsummer.

A final, and in some respects even more interesting, example of variation in flower numbers is round-headed bush clover. Seeds for this rather delicate yet prominent plant were sown with the rest when the prairie was first established, but it was not until the sixth year after planting the prairie that these plants were first spotted, and even then there were only a handful.

That's only half the story, though. Eight years after the original seeding, more seeds were sown to add plant diversity to the backyard prairie. All the seeds we added but one were of new plants. Because we felt

Prairie blazing star, a late-summer bloomer, was conspicuous in the backyard prairie the first few years but has become increasingly rare over time. We believe that prairie voles may have been eating the corms—the thickened, underground stems that store nutrients.

Above, *rattlesnake master is another plant that has shown variation in abundance throughout the years since the backyard prairie was first planted. It did not flower during the first few years, but once it began to do so, it bloomed in profusion. Fifteen years after the planting of the backyard prairie, rattlesnake master was among the most abundant plants, probably helped along by successful seeding of existing plants. This species also does well after fire.* Right, *the small and delicately beautiful flowers of round-headed bush clover make this legume a favorite late-summer bloomer in the prairie. It was slow to get started, not blooming until seven years after its initial planting.*

39

round-headed bush clover was an attractive plant, we wanted to try to establish a more robust population, so we included seeds for round-headed bush clover in the new seeding. The results were beyond anything we had any reasonable hope for.

By the third year after this new seeding, we began to see quite a few of these plants, and by the sixth year, round-headed bush clover was growing in profusion. Why it should have grown so well from the second seeding but not from the first is not at all clear. Obviously, the surrounding plants were completely different in the first few years of the backyard prairie than they were when additional seeds were sown, but whether this had any effect is impossible to say. Maybe there was a difference in viability or germination between batches of seeds. There is no doubt whatsoever that this little drama of plant proliferation is only one of a cornucopia of mysteries that keep us enthralled year after year.

Quite beyond the lessons to be learned from an observation of variations in numbers of plants, every prairie has a wonderful diversity of attractions for expert and casual observer alike. Take color, for instance. Even in a few acres like the backyard prairie, we are continually astonished

Yellow compass plant flowers stand out against a background of violet showy tick trefoil and wild bergamot in the foreground. In the background, you can also see the yellow flowers of a few false sunflowers. Color like this makes the backyard prairie a wonderful spectacle throughout the summer and into the fall.

A view of the backyard prairie during summer reveals an array of colors. Here the predominant colors are white (from rattlesnake master), purple (lower right, prairie blazing star), and yellow (rosinweed, center; false sunflower, lower right; and gray-headed coneflowers, center, with dark heads and drooping yellow petals).

and delighted at the riot of colors that appear every summer. Brilliant yellow, bright white, deep red, vivid violet, and all manner of greens and browns are only a few of the colors to be seen. What makes the spectacle all the more entrancing is that not all the flowers bloom at the same time. Further, some plants show their flowers for only a few weeks, while others last for several months. Each spiderwort flower lasts only a few hours! The result is that for six months, from May through October, it seems as if each week brings a different mix of colors as new buds open and old ones die back to produce seeds.

And that's just the large, showy plants. Hidden among these are many small, colorful wildflowers that are not immediately apparent at first glance. Only a few feet high, purple prairie clover enlivens the summer scene, sporting its namesake color. We can also see the bright scarlet flowers of royal catchfly. In the fall, we find the delicate white-flowered heath aster. Finding one of these small flowers, scattered in the prairie like hidden gems, is a reward for looking closely among the taller plants.

Everyone loves a beautiful flower, and we are no different. When we looked carefully at the flowers in the backyard prairie, we found not only the obvious differences in color and size but also an incredibly rich variety of structure. Take the beautiful and simple flowers of spiderwort. Three blue-violet petals make a pretty backdrop to the pistil and bright yellow anthers in the middle of the flower. This, then, is a typical flower in many respects. All the parts can readily be seen.

The flowers of Culver's root and rattlesnake master are not so simple. The white flowers of these plants are small and grouped into clusters, Culver's root flowers sitting on a spikelike stalk and rattlesnake master flowers forming a sphere that resembles a small, spiny golf ball. Look closely and you can see the individual flowers that make up the spike and the ball. These small individual flowers are not all that different from the large flowers of spiderwort, since both share the basic pistil, anther, and petal structure.

Contrast this with more complex flowers, like the ones known as composites. This is an enormous group that includes daisies, sunflowers, asters, and their relatives. The flower of a New England aster, for example, looks at first glance like a typical flower similar to the spiderwort except for having many petals rather than just three. However, closer examination reveals the astonishing fact that what most people identify as the "flower" actually consists of a myriad of small individual flowers. The ones on the periphery have a single "petal" each, whereas the ones inside this peripheral circle have no petals that are obvious to the eye. These "disk" flowers do indeed have petals, but these petals are fused into a tiny tube that encloses the pistil and anthers.

It's easy to be so taken with the flowers in a prairie that you tend to ignore everything else. We admit to this bias ourselves occasionally as we stroll through the prairie. There is another aspect, though, of even a small prairie that is just about impossible to overlook—the height of some prairie plants. Unlike most garden flowers, which have a comforting human scale, many prairie plants are *very* tall. By late summer, the flower stalks of compass plant and prairie dock tower well over your head. Big bluestem and Indian grass are nearly as tall. This surprises and delights some first-time visitors to the backyard prairie. It is astonishing to think that all this lush growth happens in just one season.

On next page: Top row, left, *purple prairie clover can often be found hiding among prairie grasses. This summer bloomer might be only two or three feet tall and can be difficult to spot among the taller plants. Its brilliant purple flower head, however, is striking and worth the time to search out. The yellow-petaled flower in the background is black-eyed Susan.* Center, *among the plants that are not especially tall, royal catchfly adds a splash of vibrant red to the backyard prairie.* Right, *heath aster is a common prairie plant that blooms in late summer to early fall. Its delicate white flowers can be found low among the tall grasses of a prairie, but visitors who wish to see them must look diligently.* Bottom row, left, *the blue-violet flowers of Ohio spiderwort are simple and beautiful. Brightly colored anthers in the center of the flower lend an attractive splash of yellow that can be appreciated by those who look at it closely. Each one opens in the early morning, but by midafternoon the petals wilt and dissolve into a jellylike fluid.* Right, *a close-up view of the delicate and complex flowers of Culver's root reveals details not seen at a distance.*

Above right, *the tiny flowers of rattlesnake master form a tightly packed sphere that looks like a spiny golf ball.* Right, *the blossoms of New England aster are reminiscent of traditional garden flowers. This might look like one flower, but in reality, what you see is a composite: the central head actually consists of many individual tiny flowers. It blooms in early fall and is a favorite of bees and butterflies.*

44

The flowering stems of compass plants tower over the backyard prairie on a summer afternoon. They can easily reach a height of eight feet.

45

When we look at our backyard prairie and concentrate on the flowers, another essential part of the prairie is easy to ignore—grass. But prairie isn't prairie without grass. In fact, it is estimated that as much as 80 percent of the biomass (the total mass of plant materials) in tallgrass prairie is grass.

In selecting plants for the backyard prairie, we picked many more wildflowers than grasses, probably proportionately more than might be found in another planting. But we did not neglect the grasses by any means. Grass not only is a necessary part of a healthy prairie but also has many aesthetic qualities in its own right.

Indian grass can easily reach heights of eight feet, but even in midsummer before it reaches that height, gazing at Indian grass can be mesmerizing. There's something about watching the leaves waving gently in the

Indian grass is one of the common grasses in tallgrass prairie. The featherlike heads emerge in late summer. It was probably the mesmerizing sight of this grass waving in the breeze that inspired early explorers to compare the open prairie to the ocean.

breeze that attracts the eye and the mind. In late summer and early fall, the featherlike tops of Indian grass are even more attractive as they wave in the breeze. This may well be why early explorers often compared the prairie to the ocean and were apprehensive about crossing it.

Indian grass is not the only characteristic grass of tallgrass prairie. Little bluestem, more delicate in appearance and shorter in stature than Indian grass, and its taller brother big bluestem are iconic grasses of tallgrass prairie. The slender aspect of big bluestem makes it look more ephemeral than the robust Indian grass.

Whether we are looking at the flowers or the grasses, we often revel in the details as we gaze on our prairie. One of the real joys of the backyard prairie is the pleasure to be found in looking closely at something as seemingly simple as a stalk of grass. On a dewy morning, the beauty of dewdrops on prairie grass is hard to beat. And walking through the backyard prairie after a late-summer shower is a treat not to be missed. The rainbow of colors presented by prairie flowers may be the prairie's main attraction, but we have found that small details like these enhance any prairie experience.

Big bluestem is a defining grass of tallgrass prairie. The three pronged "turkey foot" seed heads rise on stems to six feet or more by late summer. Big bluestem and its cousin little bluestem grow in clumps that turn an attractive russet brown in the winter.

CHAPTER 5

SIX LEGS AND EIGHT

Among the novel discomforts of the West, that of insects is one of no trifling character. The whole earth and air seems teeming with them, and mosquitoes, gallinippers, bugs, ticks, sand-flies, sweat-flies, house-flies, ants, cockroaches, etc., join in one continued attack against one's ease.   —William Oliver, 1843

It was a beautiful summer day when I spotted it. Large and brightly colored, it was a showy eastern tiger swallowtail butterfly. Bigger than the familiar monarch, it had striking yellow wings with sharply contrasting black stripes that made it easy to identify, even from a distance. A slow and stealthy approach allowed me to get close enough that I could just make out the long proboscis, acting like a straw as the insect sucked up nectar. Not too close, though. The swallowtail was a nervous feeder and took off again before I could draw near. Nevertheless, as it flitted from flower to flower looking for more sugary treats, I marveled again at the natural beauty that even a small patch of prairie could reveal.

As evident from William Oliver's observation, the historic prairie must have been crawling and buzzing with an astonishing diversity of life. Fortunately, the backyard prairie is rarely visited by the biting flies described by early travelers, for which we can certainly be thankful. But there are other visitors.

The tiger swallowtail is only one of many hundreds of kinds of what some people just refer to as bugs that have graced our prairie with their presence. In fact, one of the real joys of watching the maturation of the backyard prairie has been seeing the variety of such animals that are attracted to it. Butterflies, dragonflies, and a never-ending parade of other

A black-and-gold bumble bee feeds on white wild indigo in early summer.

insects can be found by a patient visitor. Spiders are also present—large ones, small ones, orb web weavers, stealthy stalkers, and other kinds that call the prairie home. It's as if the insects and spiders are manifesting the (paraphrased) famous quote from actor Kevin Costner in the movie *Field of Dreams*, "Build it and they will come." That definitely seems to be the case with the backyard prairie.

Butterflies like the tiger swallowtail are the most obvious insects that visit the prairie. Black swallowtails, buckeyes, painted ladies, and the iconic monarch can all be found through the spring, summer, and fall in the prairie. While just watching them is pleasure enough, for the careful observer, there's more to their presence than simply their beauty.

As the plants in flower change over the course of the seasons from spring to fall, so do the types of butterflies. In the spring, mourning cloak and red admiral butterflies are among the first to appear. By late June and July, we see plenty of cabbage whites and black swallowtails. It's not only the large and showy butterflies that come and go through the season. By midsummer, many small butterflies, such as the pearl crescent, eastern tailed-blue, and little yellow, have made an appearance. As summer fades

Brightly colored and easy to recognize, eastern tiger swallowtail butterflies are frequent visitors to the flowers in the backyard prairie throughout the summer.

Above left, *in early September, a painted lady butterfly enjoys nectar from stiff goldenrod flowers.* Left, *though harder to spot, small butterflies like this eastern tailed-blue, with a wingspan of about an inch, are striking enough to make finding them worth the effort. The name comes from the bright blue of the upper sides of the wings, sides that are rarely seen in this butterfly when it is resting, since it keeps its wings together above its back.*

51

into fall, another set of visitors becomes apparent, such as buckeyes and red-spotted purples.

One colorful butterfly we see throughout the summer and fall is the monarch. This icon of the prairie, the object of countless articles and books, is surely the best-known and most beloved butterfly in North America. Its striking orange and black colors and dramatic thousand-mile migration from the United States and Canada to Mexico and back have captured the attention of generations of nature lovers. Monarchs seen in the late spring are migrants returning to feeding grounds in the United States and Canada from Mexico. These migrating butterflies mate and lay eggs as they move northward. A second and then a third generation grows up where these eggs are laid, until finally in late fall, a fourth generation emerges and migrates back to Mexico.

Monarchs make a wonderful and colorful feature of any prairie but hidden in plain sight among the monarchs is the viceroy, a little-known look-alike that with luck and a keen eye you might be able to find. It is smaller than the monarch and has a black bar across each hind wing, but that's not much to go on if you only see the insect from a distance. It looks so much like the monarch that you really have to be near it to see the difference. In this similarity lies an interesting facet of natural history.

Compared with most wildlife, insects are small, numerous, and widespread. All of them can easily wind up as someone else's meal. Different

A monarch butterfly feeds on stiff goldenrod in the fall before continuing on its journey to Mexico.

A viceroy butterfly, identified by the curving black band on the hind wing, pretends to be a monarch. These butterflies appear only late in the summer and are never as numerous as the monarchs they mimic.

insects have different strategies to avoid such a fate. Some are cryptic and hard to spot against their natural background, like moths that rest on trees. Others advertise their defensive systems, like black-and-yellow-striped bees and wasps. Monarchs also advertise, but in this case they are advertising poison. As caterpillars, they eat milkweed leaves, which contain a toxic chemical. The toxin does the young caterpillars and adult butterflies no harm but is extremely distasteful to birds and mammals, which learn to avoid eating the monarchs.

All well and good for the monarch. But what about the viceroy? Here is where a bit of trickery comes in. Most insects that closely resemble each other are also closely related evolutionarily. Viceroys, however, are in a different taxonomic group from monarchs and in fact are most closely related to butterflies that look nothing at all like monarchs.

53

Then why the similarity to monarchs? This is the tricky part. The caterpillars of viceroy butterflies do not feed on milkweed, but they do feed on other plants containing chemicals that render both the caterpillar and the adult quite distasteful to birds. Viceroys could have evolved their own separate warning coloration. Each year, young birds would then have had to learn not only that monarchs are distasteful but that viceroys are as well.

By mimicking the appearance of a monarch, viceroy butterflies share with monarchs the risk that a young bird will try to eat one. Because each fledgling bird has to learn only one warning color, fewer monarchs and viceroys are sacrificed, hence benefiting both species.

Dragonflies also frequent the backyard prairie in profusion. We have counted nearly a dozen different species so far, including the striking Carolina saddlebags. This is a bit surprising, because all dragonfly nymphs (immature young) are aquatic, living in ponds or slow-moving streams until they molt into adults after one or more years. The adults are therefore usually found near water. However, adults will range several miles from water to feed, and both standing and running water can be found within a

The Carolina saddlebags dragonfly is one of over a dozen species of dragonflies that have visited our backyard prairie. Dragonfly nymphs live in water, but there is no year-round standing water in the backyard prairie, so it's not clear where this one spent its youth. Dragonflies prey on small insects, and they likely find plenty of food in the backyard prairie.

A jagged ambush bug lurks on a false sunflower, hoping for a meal. The potential meal is a flying ant. Although carnivorous, jagged ambush bugs only eat other insects and will not attack humans, though they might bite if picked up.

few miles of the backyard prairie. Furthermore, in the spring or fall, some of the dragonflies we see may be migrants returning from or flying to their overwintering grounds.

Even if you have a great fondness for insects, you must admit that although most are rather innocuous, some can be downright scary. Or at least scary looking. Consider the jagged ambush bug. This is quite a small insect, less than half an inch long. Although it is predatory and will eat anything it can catch, it is harmless to humans because of its small size. If you're like me, you might enjoy spotting one sitting on a flower waiting for lunch to drop by. If you don't think that's your thing, don't worry. Since they are small, they are also hard to see, so you can easily walk by one and not notice it at all.

For many people, praying mantises also fall into the category of being a bit scary looking. The backyard prairie is home to two different kinds of praying mantises. The large Chinese mantis (adults can reach four inches in length) was accidentally introduced to North America from Asia in 1896 and is thriving here. The smaller Carolina mantis (adults are only two inches in length), on the other hand, has been in North America for millions of years. Don't expect color to help you in distinguishing these insects. Individuals in both species can range from bright green to a striped grayish-brown. At a glance, size is a better determinant of species.

Praying mantises gained their popular name from their characteristic pose, sitting upright with the two front legs folded against the body as if praying. They could as easily be called "preying" mantises, though, because they are ambush predators, and what they're really doing is waiting for another insect to come along so they can eat it.

If you're lucky—and patient—you might be able to see a praying mantis in action. Look for the adults in late summer or early fall, as they sit quietly on or near a flower. If you get close, the mantis will often move its head to follow your movements. With its large eyes and extremely mobile head, it seems almost human. Especially if you are not a devotee of horror films, an insect that looks as though it is watching you can be a bit creepy.

Left, *a Chinese mantis observes the photographer. These nonnative insects are quite large, at three to four inches long, so a Chinese mantis can be unsettling to see, especially since it will move its head to keep an eye on you. Fortunately, they do not attack or bite humans, even if handled.* On opposite page, above, *a Carolina mantis has spotted a honey bee (right) and is orienting itself for a strike. This native species of mantis is much smaller than the similar-looking Chinese mantis.* Right, *the mantis, having caught the bee, begins to eat it immediately. The strike of the mantis when it catches prey is so fast it appears almost instantaneous to the human eye.*

When some unsuspecting insect drops by to eat pollen or drink nectar, the mantis slowly and carefully orients its body to point at what it sees as lunch, and then, faster than a blink, shoots out its forelegs to catch the unlucky insect. The meal begins immediately, while the hapless victim struggles helplessly. Life on the prairie is not always pretty.

Spiders might also seem creepy, but a healthy prairie does not exist without them. Ours is no exception. Crab spiders and jumping spiders, like praying mantises, are hunters that sit and wait to pounce on unsuspecting prey. Jumping spiders are alert to their surroundings, so you might even see one peer up at you as it waits for lunch on the petal of a flower.

Orb-weaving spiders provide a special treat for the eyes, weaving beautifully intricate and ornate webs. We see these webs throughout much of the year, but the fall is when they really come into their own. In September, we delight in seeing the one- to two-foot-diameter webs that are spun by the large black-and-yellow orb weavers called banded garden spiders. These two-inch-long predators wait patiently in the centers of their beautiful webs to catch their next meal. Not a fan of spiders? Not to worry. These

Above, *a crab spider, so named for its unusually long, crablike legs, patiently waits for an unsuspecting insect to drop by. Left, a crab spider has captured its prey, a fly visiting the daisy flower to eat pollen or sip nectar. No doubt the fly did not think it was going to be the meal.*

spiders and their webs are large enough to be spotted from a distance, so you can easily avoid them. Even if you do happen to stumble across one accidentally, the spider will scuttle away, much more afraid of you than you are of it. Quell your anxiety and take a look. You may be surprised at the beauty of these creatures.

Not every interaction in our backyard prairie is blood and guts. Various bees, both bumble bees and solitary bees, also began to frequent the backyard prairie as it matured. Bumble bees are always entertaining to watch. They feed on nectar and collect pollen for their developing young, so they can be seen on many of the prairie flowers that bloom from mid to late summer. Some people are concerned about bees and wasps of any type, thinking that they may be stung. Although bumble bees can sting, they are not aggressive. As long as I watch them and do not disturb their pollen gathering, they pose no threat—even when I get close enough to take photographs.

Just as the types of butterflies that can be seen in the backyard prairie vary with the time of year, so also does the presence of other insects. This is perhaps most striking with grasshoppers and katydids. In the spring and summer, the backyard prairie is rather quiet, the silence broken only by the rustle of plants disturbed by wind or the occasional singing of birds. Fall is a different story, however, full of the loud cacophony of chirps and trills produced by crickets and katydids. They're not singing for our benefit. The

Far left, *a spiderweb glistens in the morning dew. Round webs like this are woven by a group of spiders appropriately enough called orb weavers. By September, the prairie is often filled with orb webs, each one strung between two tall prairie plants.* Left, *banded garden spiders such as this one are among the spiders that spin large orb webs in the prairie. Large enough to be seen readily (bodies of females can be up to an inch long), these spiders add a colorful accent to the fall prairie. They are also a good reason to stay on the walking paths in the fall!*

59

sounds you hear are made by males advertising their presence and trying to attract females. Each species makes its own unique pattern of sound, and the females are attuned to the sounds of the males of that particular species. You may be astonished to learn that the sounds we can hear are usually only a small part of the repertoire that these insects produce; many insects produce songs that contain notes at a pitch far too high for the human ear to hear.

I have never seen a cricket or katydid actually singing, but that's not surprising. They are usually hidden in the thick vegetation and are alert to predators. They stop singing at the approach of a human. But if you were lucky enough to see one singing, you might be surprised to see that legs may not be involved at all. A common misconception is that crickets sing by rubbing their two hind legs together. Not true.

A black-and-gold bumble bee sips nectar from the flower of wild bergamot. The bee in this case does not actually fully alight on the flower but sips while hovering.

60

Sound is produced in different ways by different insects, but for crickets and katydids, the wings are always involved. The insect either rubs its two wings together, as do many crickets, or rubs a hind leg rapidly against a wing. The wings are adapted to produce vibrations from a specialized section, hence producing the sound. It's just as well that you don't need to know anything at all about how this is done to enjoy the symphony. Jamie is particularly fond of walking through the backyard prairie on a sunny day in late summer or early fall to enjoy the amazing symphony of sound. It's another reminder that even small patches of prairie are teeming with life.

A tree cricket is silhouetted by sunlight filtering through the leaf of a compass plant.

CHAPTER 6

FEATHERS AND FUR

Squirrels, raccoons, foxes, deer, wolves, and bears abound; as do wild turkeys and quails; geese and ducks partially; hawks, buzzards, and pigeons in tolerable quantities.
—Henry Bradshaw Fearon, 1819

It was a special moment. On a calm, sunny late-winter morning, there it was, loping along our prairie trail—a coyote. Nearly hidden in the prairie grasses, it cruised by casually, completely oblivious to the excited observers in the nearby house.

It was not the first time we had seen a coyote in our prairie, but sightings of these normally nocturnal animals are not common. They could

Left, *a white-tailed deer stands near a path through a prairie park.* Right, *an uncommon sight, this coyote lopes through a farm field adjacent to the backyard prairie on a winter day. You may just be able to make out the small animal, likely a rabbit, it is carrying in its mouth.*

certainly be heard at night, especially when an emergency vehicle sped by with sirens blaring. We always knew when an ambulance was coming, because the coyotes started howling long before we could hear anything and continued for some time after the sound had faded away from our ears.

Tracks are always plentiful, though. Every winter in the morning after a snowfall, we are delighted to see footprints of coyotes on the walking trails in our prairie. We imagine them thinking to themselves, "I don't know where these paths came from, but I'm sure going to use them as long as they're here!"

In contrast to the mostly unseen coyote, the most visible animals on the open prairie historically were bison. The million-strong herds of these magnificent animals that roamed the prairies, even into Illinois, are long

gone. The only places to see bison now, apart from zoos or private farms, are national parks like Yellowstone or large-scale prairie restorations like Nachusa Grasslands. Impressive as they are, the several thousand bison to be found there pale in comparison to the herds that, according to travelers, would sometimes take days to pass a single spot.

Early explorers who traversed the prairie and later settlers who stayed reported an abundance of animals in and around prairies. These included game animals, such as bison, deer, and elk; predators, such as cougars, wolves, and coyotes; and smaller mammals, such as raccoons, opossums, skunks, snakes, and ground squirrels. By the time Illinois became a state in 1818, even with only around 12,000 people of European descent living there, visitors reported that the bison were gone, having been hunted and having moved away from areas in which people were settling. Elk disappeared shortly thereafter, though this was probably the result of overhunting and loss of habitat rather than avoidance of European settlers. Of the large game animals, only white-tailed deer thrived after settlers began arriving and the prairie was plowed for agriculture. This may have been because their major predators, cougars and wolves, were hunted to extinction as the tallgrass prairie was settled and they adapted well to living in a landscape altered by human activity.

As described earlier, the mix of plants that we see in the backyard prairie has changed a bit over the years since it was first planted. The kinds of animals we see, however, haven't changed much. We don't have bison or elk, which is probably a good thing. But raccoons and opossums have taken advantage of the nearby woods and are seen regularly. Other animals that we expected to see in a prairie, though, were not apparent. Foxes and skunks, to take just two examples, were reported to live in and around the prairie by early travelers, but we never saw any in the backyard prairie. We thought this was because our prairie was small and separated from other natural areas by roads and farm fields, but the purchase of a trail camera that could take pictures at night without disturbing the animals proved us wrong; we've photographed both foxes and skunks.

The only large animals we see are white-tailed deer, which visit us occasionally. We sometimes see them at dawn or dusk looking for food. In the summer, they like to eat the leaves of wildflowers and seem well adapted to living near humans. Because deer usually seek forest cover for at least part of the day, there may have been few out on the open prairie away from forests historically, but in today's landscape, deer are nearly ubiquitous. We often find "beds," small areas in the prairie where the grasses and

After a snowfall, coyote tracks are a common sight on the path through the backyard prairie. Coyotes tend to move through during the night.

65

wildflowers are matted down, compacted by the presence of some large animal. Many of these beds are too large to have been made by coyotes, so we surmise that a deer may have spent part of a day or night sleeping there.

Smaller animals abound in the prairie but are harder to see. An exception is the cottontail rabbit. These relatively small mammals may vex gardeners, but they easily make a living in the backyard prairie. There is plenty of vegetation for food and cover. The dense grass also makes a perfect hiding place for kits in the spring. We have found that over the years, the rabbits have readily moved from the garden out into the prairie—though that does not inhibit them from eating garden flowers as well!

The accounts of early travelers through the prairie mention many smaller animals, such as ground squirrels and snakes. We know these animals still live in Illinois, but we have seen neither in our prairie. We assume this is mainly because of the lack of suitable habitat and nearby natural areas that contain these animals. It could also be that they are there but we just have not seen them yet. Isolation apparently has not been a problem for toads, which we do indeed see occasionally, both in the prairie and in the adjacent woods.

Of course, there are very small mammals present. I have seen no accounts of mice or voles in any writings of early visitors or settlers, but these animals were certainly present back then. They are present now as well. Maybe it's just my love of all things pertaining to nature and natural areas, but I must admit to experiencing a bit of pleasure whenever I see a vole or mouse scurrying across the path through the prairie as I walk. We also take quiet delight to see the tracks and tunnels these small mammals make in snow during the winter.

Birds are usually much more obvious denizens of the prairie, since they can be both seen and heard. Some birds, like eastern meadowlarks, eat insects or spiders and dine on the profusion of these animals throughout a prairie. Others, like American goldfinches and pine siskins, are seedeaters and will love even a small prairie for the food it provides. Then there are birds, like song sparrows and red-winged blackbirds, that are opportunistic, eating insects during the breeding season, then switching to seeds later in the year.

We have seen many of these birds through the years, but not all that could potentially be here. Therein lies another difference between the prairie as it was and prairies today, especially small ones like the backyard prairie. Early explorers and settlers remarked on many birds, but the ones they noticed were game birds like grouse and prairie chickens. These, along with many of the small birds that inhabited the prairie, are long gone.

They require large expanses of unbroken prairie, and today's environment is not big enough or wild enough to sustain them. Unfortunately, we will never see prairie chickens or grouse in the backyard prairie.

Other birds abound, however. Red-winged blackbirds readily build nests even in small prairies. We have a good-sized colony. What makes red-winged blackbirds especially interesting is that they are quite territorial, especially in the spring when they are raising their young. You can't miss these birds during a springtime walk through the backyard prairie. They like to perch on old stalks of compass plant or prairie dock, mouths agape as they give their raucous warning cries. If you get too close, they may fly overhead, trying to warn you away.

A disconcerting part of this behavior is that a bird often flies just above and behind your head. It seems to understand where your eyes are and that your eyes must be pointed at it for you to see it. If you turn around to find the noisy pest, it will fly around so that it stays behind your head. This kind of behavior may not be what you want to encounter in your backyard prairie, but the birds won't actually hurt you. You can relax and enjoy the thrilling interaction with this charismatic bird.

On opposite page, above, a cottontail rabbit looks around on the path through the backyard prairie. The rabbit feeds on tender shoots and leaves of plants; it might also make a fine meal for a coyote. Left, spring brings many birds back to the prairie, including this song sparrow. Some birds do stay through the winter, but most denizens of the prairie fly south when the days shorten. Right, a male red–winged blackbird gives its warning call. These striking and noisy birds stake out their territory in the spring and vigorously protest any intrusion to what they consider their space.

Red-winged blackbirds may be aggressive toward more than just humans. We had often seen and heard dickcissels in the rural area around the backyard prairie. Two years ago, we finally saw one or two sitting and singing in the prairie. That summer was the last we saw of them in the prairie, however. We saw frequent instances of a red-winged blackbird chasing a dickcissel away. Although we don't know for sure, it's easy to imagine that the aggressive red-winged blackbirds were more than the smaller dickcissel wanted to deal with. The dickcissels are still abundant in the surrounding agricultural land, but in areas that are not frequented by red-winged blackbirds.

Large raptors, such as Cooper's hawks and red-tailed hawks, also frequent our prairie and the surrounding fields, soaring high as they circle in the air looking for inattentive birds or small mammals for their next meals. If you have a place for them to perch, like a tree, a bird feeder, or even a weather station, you may also see them surveying their surroundings, looking for lunch! Sometimes we find the remains of a bird—bits of feather, flesh, and bones—that likely was from a hawk's meal.

Birds that migrate through central Illinois, such as pine siskins, frequently stop at the backyard prairie to rest and find food as they pass through in the spring or fall on their way to summer nesting grounds or overwintering sites. Other migrants, like American goldfinches, may

Above left, a male red-winged blackbird hovers over the head of an intruder, the photographer in this case, near its nest. On opposite page, a male dickcissel sings in the prairie. Red-winged blackbirds are as aggressive toward these birds as they are to humans and often chase them away. Dickcissels would likely nest in the backyard prairie if not for the blackbirds.

arrive in the spring and stay throughout the summer. In the fall, they gorge themselves on the abundant seeds available in the prairie in preparation for the trip south for the winter. Fall goldfinches don't sport the brilliant black and yellow feathers apparent during mating season, but their cheerful chirps and undulating flight as they go from flower to flower looking for seed are enchanting nevertheless. So even before and after the balmy days of summer, we walk through our prairie with a bird book in hand and see what we can find.

A Cooper's hawk finds a weathervane an opportune spot from which to look for lunch. Small birds that normally congregate on the nearby bird feeder vanish when this predator is in the vicinity.

Above, *a pine siskin enjoys a repast of seeds from stiff goldenrod in preparation for its fall migration.* Right, *as fall approaches, an American goldfinch feasts on the seeds of rosinweed in the backyard prairie.*

CHAPTER 7

SEASONS

Seasons came and went; tender spring, glowing summer, ripening autumn, stern winter; and in them all was wondrous beauty of impressive majesty! —Eliza Farnham, 1846

Frost on the backyard prairie was nothing new (it was January, after all), but this was just surreal. The temperature had dropped overnight from above freezing to somewhere in the 20s Fahrenheit, wringing moisture out of the air and depositing it as frost on every available surface. What made this frost unique was that a strong wind had been blowing during

Left, *frost covers the top of showy goldenrod after a freezing night in December.* Right, *frost covers the stalks of prairie plants on a winter's morning. A cold strong wind overnight caused ice crystals to form predominantly on one side.*

73

the night, causing the ice crystals to line up on the downwind side of each stem and leaf across the prairie. The entire scene was like something out of a fantasy novel, someone's idea of an otherworldly landscape.

Midwestern winter days are short and often dreary with clouds. It's cold. And snow, while often pretty just after it falls, poses challenges for those trying to get around.

As the frost story suggests, however, winter on a prairie is a different matter altogether. True enough, the riot of color we enjoyed from the

In this panoramic view of the prairie in the winter, everything is lifeless in the snow and cold aboveground, but underground the prairie plants are waiting patiently for spring.

spring to the fall is long gone. Prairie plants lie dormant, conserving their resources until the weather warms again. The backyard prairie looks dead and lifeless, dull brown and gray with perhaps some snow thrown in for contrast. But that doesn't mean there's nothing to see.

Take that snow, for example. I might complain about having to shovel it off the driveway, but before I do, I head out to the prairie. I put on my boots, bundle up in warm clothes, and venture out after a snowfall. It's not unusual for snow to drift across open spaces in the prairie. The dead

stalks of prairie plants act like wind breaks, causing snow to accumulate near them. Even with only a few inches of snowfall, drifts may well reach a depth of several feet. These drifts are impressive not only because of their size but also because the wind often sculpts them into interesting shapes.

Snow also serves as a great contrast to the browns and grays of prairie plants. The distinctive leaf of a compass plant, for example, makes a striking contrast against a white snow background. And after a snowfall, many of the dead plant stalks wind up sporting small snow caps.

Flowering plants have several ways to survive winter. Annuals are plants that live only a single season. They produce thousands, sometimes millions, of seeds, and those seeds lie dormant in the soil ready to germinate when conditions are right in the spring or summer to produce the next generation.

Most prairie plants, though, are perennials. Parts of these plants simply die back when the days shorten and the weather turns cold. All the above-ground foliage dies, leaving only the roots, protected deep underground, still alive. When the days lengthen and the sun warms the cold ground, the roots send up new shoots to begin the cycle all over again.

As we walk around our prairie in the winter, we often look for small details in the snow. The seed heads of wild bergamot may be sticking up just above the surface of the snow like forgotten miniature toy balls. Under

Top left, *drifted snow is often piled up by the wind, as here along a path through the prairie.* Top right, *round-headed bush clover still wears a jaunty cap of ice and snow some days after a snowfall.* Above, *a seed head of wild bergamot peeks up through the snow after a heavy snowfall.*

the right conditions, wind and plant stems may also conspire to draw interesting patterns in the snow.

Most people think there's not much life to be seen during the winter. For plants, that's certainly true. The living parts are tucked safely underground, waiting for the thaws of spring. But just because you don't see the living creatures, that doesn't mean they aren't there, nor that you can't see evidence of their activity.

The most obvious evidence of life in the winter prairie is tracks in the snow. Coyotes, especially, seem to appreciate the walking trails that wind through the backyard prairie, treating them like highways. There are plenty of smaller creatures that run across the snow as well. Some of these leave rather interesting footprints, a pleasant surprise for the winter observer. Not only can you see the many signs of small mammals, but you can sometimes also find where they live, as tracks often form paths that converge on one or two hidden spots leading to a burrow in the snow or grass.

Every year, I look forward to the longer and warmer days of spring. In addition to melting snow and ice, they bring the year's first signs of life. Small, green leaves of golden alexanders and black-eyed Susans lie mostly hidden among the dry stalks and leaves of the previous season. If I look where the snow smashed down the dead leaves and stems of last year's growth, though, I can see new leaves and stems pushing through.

Above, *the stems of a prairie grass carve out near-perfect circles in the snow as they are moved about by the wind.* Right, *a small animal's tracks in the snow cross the walking path through the prairie.*

As explained earlier, many prairies are burned in late winter or early spring. As spring progresses, new leaves come up after a fire and provide a welcome contrast to the black, gray, and brown left by the fire. By May, golden alexanders, one of the earliest-flowering prairie plants, have begun to carpet the green prairie with their yellow blooms.

By the time June arrives, spiderwort, pale purple coneflower, and other spring flowers are in full bloom, and the summer parade of color is in full swing. Throughout the season, flowers open and close in a stately order, turning the prairie into a riot of blues, yellows, and purples, all the colors of the rainbow. A multitude of colorful butterflies and bees attracted by the flowers are also looking for nectar in the prairie.

After we had observed the backyard prairie for several years, we noticed one way that prairies differ from gardens. In a garden, you either plant or tend to the same plants in the same places year after year. Prairies, however, are wild places. We saw that not all the plants in our prairie thrived every year. As we mentioned earlier, some prairie plants will take several years to grow before they send up stalks with flowers. But even after a plant has begun flowering, that doesn't mean it will flower as vigorously each year. Compass plant, for example, may bloom in profusion one year but be virtually absent, or seemingly so, the next. The plants are still

On opposite page, above left, *after a late-winter prescribed burn, it is easy to see the prairie greening up in the spring.* Above center, *a mass of bright yellow golden alexanders is a sure sign that spring has arrived. These flowers are among the very first to bloom in the backyard prairie.* Left, *this panoramic view of the prairie in the spring shows how dormant prairie plants send up green shoots once the days begin to lengthen and warm weather hits. The scattering of blue comes from the flowers of spiderwort, a spring bloomer.*

Right, *black-eyed Susan and pale purple coneflower bring a touch of color to the green of the late-spring prairie.*

Left, *the violet flower of Ohio spiderwort shows off its yellow stamens after a spring rain. Below, in this panoramic view of the prairie in the summer, most flowering prairie plants have reached their full height and provide a spectacular and colorful scene.*

there, readily identified by their distinctive leaves, but few put up the long, tall stalks on which flowers appear.

Some of this variation is a response to fire. Rattlesnake master, for example, seems to respond particularly vigorously the summer after a late-winter burn. This is not the only factor, however. The prairie experiences fluctuations in many variables throughout the year, such as excessive or not enough rainfall, an unusually snowy winter, or a cold, wet spring. Each of these factors alone or in combination may affect how likely prairie plants are to send up flowering shoots. It's one of the beauties of having a

An early fall panorama, in comparison with the summer one, shows starkly how different the prairie looks at various times of the year. In the fall, the prairie is dominated by the yellow of goldenrod flowers.

prairie of our own to be able to see the variation not only of the seasons but of the prairie itself through the years.

As summer turns to fall, the colors of the prairie turn a rich yellow. Goldenrods dominate the prairie, turning it into a bicolored green-and-yellow landscape. In addition, seeds ripen. It is delightful each fall to see birds flock to the feast these provide, preparing either for a migration to warmer climes or for the cold winter ahead. In the fall, we see pine siskins, American goldfinches, and many other birds gorging themselves on the abundant seeds the prairie produces.

Birds aren't the only migrants we see. The iconic monarch butterfly begins its thousand-mile journey back to its overwintering grounds in Mexico each fall. This migration waxes and wanes, being obvious some years and less so in others. In good years, we may see many hundreds of these colorful insects flitting about in our prairie to rest and feed for a day before continuing their journey. Some dragonflies migrate as well, though much less is known about this migration. We occasionally find on late-summer evenings that the air above the backyard prairie is filled with dragonflies. The next evening, they may be gone. In many cases, no one is quite sure where they go.

In the fall, we also notice many other small invertebrates that are now adults and large enough to be obvious—praying mantises and grasshoppers galore, as well as their spider relatives, lurking for unwary prey. The Carolina mantis can be hard to spot (even though adults are about two inches long, they blend in and sit still), but when I do see one, I take some time to observe it for a while. If I'm lucky, I can watch it catch a meal. Its lightning-fast strike is always astonishing to witness, though the subsequent meal it makes of its victim is not for the squeamish.

In the fall, migrating birds flock to the prairie to fatten up on its abundant seeds. Here an American goldfinch prepares to chow down on the seeds of rattlesnake master.

Dragonflies are silhouetted against the sunset in this photo. In late summer, hundreds of dragonflies congregate over the backyard prairie, hunting for insects en route to their southern overwintering grounds.

Above, *a Carolina mantis stalks the prairie looking for its next meal. Right, showy goldenrod, its bright yellow flowers long gone, nevertheless glows when lit by the early-morning sun on a bright November day.*

As the days shorten, the flowers disappear. Even so, we don't abandon the prairie now. The afternoon sun, now closer to the horizon than in the summer, gives a golden glow to the landscape. Morning can be magical as well, as the low sun is filtered through the seeds that have replaced the colorful flowers. In addition, many prairie plants, such as thistles, asters, and goldenrods, produce gossamer fluffs called thistledown that sail on the wind, spreading far and wide the small seeds attached like tiny parachutists.

Fall is also the time when many insects prepare for the winter. What each insect does depends on what kind of insect it is. There are two or three main adaptations to survive the cold. Some insects lay eggs in sheltered places in plant stems, under leaves, or underground. The adults die, and the eggs that survive then hatch out in the spring, starting the next generation. Some insects actually overwinter as adults, finding a sheltered place and slowing their metabolism, emerging and mating in the spring. A third pattern is for the insect to develop to the larval stage during the summer and early fall, then overwinter as a pupa, emerging as a moth or butterfly in the spring.

The cold grip of winter arrives too soon to the backyard prairie after the pleasantly crisp days of fall, but the winter and its ever-present tracks in the snow await.

Pasture thistle seeds in a prairie park await a wind to spread them far and wide.

CHAPTER 8

OPEN SKY

I do not know of any thing that struck me more forcibly than the sensation of solitude I experienced in crossing this, and some of the other large Prairies. I was perfectly alone, and could see nothing in any direction but sky and grass. —William Blane, 1824

It wasn't a tornado, but it was an impressive sight nevertheless. Not only was there the usual dark cloud signaling a rainstorm, but we could actually see dark streaks in the sky indicating the torrential downpour in the distance as rain pummeled the parched ground. Looking west from the house, we had an unobstructed view of this force of nature across the open

Left, *view of prairie and open sky.* Right, *a storm on a summer evening dumps rain on the ground several miles away. An open prairie gives unparalleled views of a distant horizon.*

89

expanse of the backyard prairie and adjacent agricultural fields. The storm was far enough distant that we were in no danger of getting wet, yet close enough to appreciate its majesty.

On the open prairie, the sky is omnipresent. A flat, rolling landscape mostly free from the obstructions of buildings and trees allows you not just to see but to experience the open sky. Forests keep secrets hidden in their dark, moist shadows, but there is little to hide—and little place to hide—on the prairie. Across the midwestern states, the tall grasses, wild-flowers, and bison might be gone, but the open sky in all its wild wonder is still there.

When we decided to plant the backyard prairie, we had some idea of the wonders of flowers, butterflies, and furry animals that we might experience. We had not, however, fully appreciated how much we would enjoy the wide-open vista of the prairie sky.

When we walk on our prairie, it's not uncommon for us to see a red-tailed hawk glide by, hunting for a meal, or turkey vultures reel and soar high above, catching the warm updrafts and riding the waves of wind. Looking out to the long horizon, we often feel like masters of all we survey. But there is admittedly also sometimes a feeling of being just two solitary humans with the dome of the world above and the prairie earth below.

This is what the first explorers and settlers must have felt when venturing out of the forests of the eastern United States onto the great grasslands of the Midwest. They compared the prairie to the sea—grasses rippling in the wind like waves on the ocean, nary a landmark in sight.

Modern visitors to prairie may find it hard to put themselves in the minds of seventeenth-century explorers and eighteenth- and nineteenth-century settlers as they encountered the prairie the first time. Many kept journals, though, that help us to understand some of their feelings. These journals describe explorers' wonder at the sight that greeted them as they ventured west out of the comforting forests they were leaving behind. Putting ourselves in their shoes, we can appreciate their apprehension. Forests were familiar. They may on occasion have been dark and foreboding, but they always provided shelter, firewood, and ready landmarks for the experienced traveler.

Prairies were something completely different. Once well away from the comforting trees, explorers found there were no landmarks or shelter. The vast expanse of sky only accentuated what must have been an over-powering sense of being completely exposed to the elements. Even Native

Puffy white clouds dot the sky across the prairie on a lazy September day. At the moment, they indicate mild weather, but these clouds could later grow to form thunderstorms.

Peoples—some of whom had been here thousands of years before explorers and settlers—tended to live, hunt, and farm in the relative comfort of forested areas. No records are left of their impressions of the prairie.

The French, who were the first Europeans to encounter the prairie and gave it its name, certainly reported their awe at the vast open spaces they encountered. But more than that, always evaluating the new land they explored for its potential as a place to live and raise crops, the early explorers deemed the prairie barren and infertile because of its lack of trees. James Monroe, writing to Thomas Jefferson about the Northwest Territory in 1786, well encapsulated the view that was common toward the end of the eighteenth century:

> *A great part of the territory is miserably poor, especially that near lakes Michigan & Erie & that upon the Mississippi & the Illinois consists of extensive plains which have not had from appearances & will not have a single bush on them, for ages.*

It seems incredible to us now, knowing as we do that the region of the tallgrass prairie contains some of the most fertile land in the world, that early settlers would have been so wrong. But fertility was associated with trees; if trees didn't grow, the thinking was, then no crop would either. There was also the practical matter of a lack of supporting resources. No trees meant no fuel for fires, no timber for houses, no wood for fences, nothing from which to construct wagons or other essentials. There was also the very practical matter of the extreme difficulty of plowing up the dense tangle of roots that made the prairie the vibrant place it actually was.

In modern times, with food and shelter only a short walk or car ride away, we can appreciate the open prairie in ways that Native Peoples, explorers, and settlers were perhaps not able to. We certainly all appreciate the open, cloudless skies that invite people out to enjoy the sunshine at any time of year. But living next to the open expanse of fields and a prairie has really made us appreciate the wonder of clouds, those often fluffy objects that can be imagined to be almost anything, in ways we never did before.

Clouds seem to come in an infinite variety of forms; indeed, over 100 types of clouds have been named. But you don't have to know the names of even the 10 basic types to appreciate the different appearances that clouds can have. Add a setting sun and you can get a spectacular show. We often walk out on our prairie near sunset to take in the view.

91

Sometimes clouds are not so comforting. In the summer, it is not unusual to see clouds begin to mass in the air in enormous formations. With a rising wind, these usually signal an impending thunderstorm. Early visitors to the open prairie often commented on the foreboding sky that signaled such a storm, as well as on the fury of the storm itself. Caught in the open, there was little they could do but hunker down and wait for it to pass. One traveler named John Regan recorded his experience in 1859:

> *Suddenly a deep booming sound came rolling over the plain, and vivid momentary pencillings of light shot athwart the dense and darkening bank of clouds. It was a thunder-storm! . . . The whole western heavens, almost to the zenith, were covered with 'blackness and darkness and tempest.' The forked lightning shot frantically from heaven to earth—the thunders uttered their most tremendous roarings, rattling and quivering in a very awe-inspiring manner."*

On opposite page, *anvil storm clouds presage a summer thunderstorm. They are beautiful from a distance.* Left, *at sunset on an April evening we observed a phenomenon called virga, rain falling from a cloud but evaporating before it reaches the ground.*

93

On opposite page, top, *high winds often presage a storm. Here pale purple coneflower petals flap in the wind that is so common in prairie. The resilient plants of the prairie are adapted to survive extreme conditions such as wind, heat, and drought.* Left, *a cumulonimbus cloud with its distinctive anvil is a good reason to seek shelter. Prairie thunderstorms can spring up quickly in the summer.* Above right, *lightning strikes can often be seen over the prairie during a thunderstorm. The wide-open prairie is a dangerous place to be in a thunderstorm, because on flat land no place is safe from lightning.*

Fortunately, we can retreat to the comfort of our house and watch a storm sweep over the prairie. Sometimes we are even treated to a spectacular light show when streaks of lightning pop and crack from cloud to ground. What we have not seen in person at the backyard prairie, which is probably a good thing, is a tornado. When conditions are right—warm, moist air wedged between masses of cold air—this most infamous weather phenomenon of the prairie sky can run free. These violent funnels of rapidly spinning air can form anywhere in North America, but they seem especially at home on the open prairie, winds up to 250 miles per hour leaving a path of destruction wherever they go. Tornadoes are fearsome and dangerous, but there's no denying that they exude a majestic power when they are seen over an open prairie.

When all the storms have passed, we are able to experience another benefit of an open prairie landscape—a beautiful sunset. Our view from the house faces west over the backyard prairie, and we really enjoy seeing the sun drop toward the horizon, down below the tall prairie grasses. And then there is the full spectacle of the sun, clouds, and a distant horizon that can take your breath away. City dwellers may occasionally be able to glimpse a lurid sky painted by the setting sun, but there's nothing like a wide horizon to allow country dwellers to enjoy the spectacle fully.

An unexpected benefit for us of having an unobstructed view of the western horizon is being able to see a variety of solar light shows besides the sunset itself. Sun pillars, for example, are shafts of light that shine like beams up to (or down from) the sun. They form when light from the sun reflects off the surfaces of ice crystals in the air. The ice crystals are associated with high, thin clouds. As the sun sinks toward the horizon, light reflects off the crystals, forming a beam visible from the ground.

Left, *a tornado is the most fearsome weather phenomenon to be encountered on the prairie. This tornado touched down in east-central Illinois in September 2016.* Photo courtesy of Jeff Frame; used by permission. Above, *the tornado in the previous image carved this path through an east-central Illinois farm field in September 2016. Fortunately for the residents of the farmstead, the tornado missed the house. Although the path is not through prairie, you can see the havoc wreaked on the crop fields. Imagine what it would do to a prairie.* Drone photo courtesy of Jeremy Wolf; used by permission.

97

Sunsets are a sight not to be missed on the open prairie, where no buildings or trees obscure the view. They are especially beautiful when clouds catch and reflect the sunlight.

Even more unusual is the occasional shadow we can see cast by a cloud. All of us are familiar with the shadows that clouds cast on the earth as they pass between us and the sun. What far fewer people ever notice is the shadow that a cloud can throw on other clouds in the evening sky as the sun nears or sinks below the horizon.

There are also the familiar sunbeams, technically known as crepuscular rays. It seems counterintuitive that rays of light from the sun, which are essentially parallel to one another, should nevertheless appear to an observer as if fanned out from a single point, but there's no denying that they exist.

Before moving out of town and establishing our backyard prairie, we might have thought, if we thought about it at all, that once the sun disappeared from view, the sky show would be over. We were wrong. The open sky is still there, and on cloudless nights, it is filled with myriad stars, planets, and the moon. Even with the naked eye, all the inner planets plus Jupiter and Saturn can easily be seen once you know where to look. A comfortable chair out on an open prairie on nights from May to September will allow you to watch the movements of the planets through the night sky. Of course, you can see the planets during other months as well, but cold weather is not conducive to stargazing!

Our moon is the most obvious and recognizable object in the night sky. The moon, waxing and waning in its leisurely 28-day cycle, is familiar to everyone. But it is a special treat for us to be out on our backyard prairie on

Above left, *a sun pillar lights up a winter's evening sky. Sun pillars are vertical shafts of light that extend from a bright light source such as the sun. They are caused by ice crystals drifting in the upper atmosphere. Above, sunbeams peek out from behind clouds near sunset. The view across the backyard prairie is never dull.*

the night of a full moon and gaze in wonder at its still-mysterious surface. As you look at the moon yourself, you can even enjoy a good mystery. When you see the moon just as it rises over the horizon, or just before it sets again, you will probably notice that it appears much larger than it does when it is high overhead. The moon doesn't actually change size; it just appears to do so. The phenomenon is real, but scientists are still not in agreement as to why it occurs at all. The open prairie is also a good spot from which to observe a total eclipse of the moon when it happens every few years.

From small partridge pea flowers to giant compass plants, from insects so tiny you can barely see them to praying mantises as big as your hand, even the small backyard prairie contains wonders beyond most people's experience. From the joy of a bright, sunny day to the mysterious feeling of a foggy morning, being out on prairie, even one as small as the backyard prairie, can be a soul-satisfying experience. Even if you don't have the space or resources to plant your own prairie, visit one near you. Whether you want to enjoy the feeling of being close to nature or to feel the grandeur of the universe by looking up into the sky, prairie affords a wonderful way to experience the natural world. We hope our observations and the photos in this book have inspired you to join us in this adventure.

The mystery of the prairie is evoked on a foggy morning in April. One might imagine that the backyard prairie continues almost endlessly beyond the lone bur oak. We know it is just farm fields and houses, but we can take solace in this small space of biodiversity and beauty we call our own.

FURTHER READING

SOURCES

FURTHER READING

If you wish to learn more about prairies, visit a prairie, or establish a prairie of your own, you can find many resources available to help. Here we list what we consider some of the most useful or interesting sources.

Adelman, Charlotte, and Bernard L. Schwartz. *Prairie Directory of North America: The United States, Canada, and Mexico*. 2nd ed. Oxford: Oxford University Press, 2013.
> A comprehensive source for finding North American public prairies, grasslands, and savannas.

Crosby, Cindy. *The Tallgrass Prairie: An Introduction*. Evanston, IL: Northwestern University Press, 2017.
> A slim but engaging introduction to the delights of tallgrass prairie.

Helzer, Chris. *The Ecology and Management of Prairies in the Central United States*. Iowa City, IA: University of Iowa Press, 2010.
> A good book for someone who has established a prairie.

Kurtz, Carl. *A Practical Guide to Prairie Reconstruction*. 2nd ed. Iowa City: University of Iowa Press, 2013.
> A good how-to book for someone thinking about establishing a prairie.

Kurtz, Don. *Prairie Wildflowers: A Guide to Flowering Plants from the Midwest to the Great Plains*. Lanham, MD: Rowman & Littlefield, 2019.
> A guide to identifying the most common flowers and grasses in a tallgrass prairie.

Ladd, Doug. *Tallgrass Prairie Wildflowers: A Field Guide to Common Wildflowers and Plants of the Midwest*. 2nd ed. Guilford, CT: Globe Pequot Press, 2005.
> Another guide to identifying the most common flowers and grasses in a tallgrass prairie.

Madson, John. *Where the Sky Began: Land of the Tallgrass Prairie*. 1982. Reprint, Iowa City: University of Iowa Press, 2004.

A discussion of the geological and human history of prairie, including consideration of its natural history.

Madson, John, and Frank Oberle. *Tallgrass Prairie*. Helena, MT: Falcon Press, 1993.

A beautiful and lyrical book that provides a wonderful introduction to tallgrass prairie.

Manning, Richard. *Grassland: The History, Biology, Politics and Promise of the American Prairie*. New York: Penguin Books, 1997.

A book that provides a thorough discussion of the wider history and politics of prairie.

Meszaros, Gary, and Guy L. Denny. *The Prairie Peninsula*. Kent, OH: Kent State University Press, 2017.

A sumptuous description of tallgrass prairie, with photographs.

Moul, Francis, and Georg Joutras. *The National Grasslands: A Guide to America's Undiscovered Treasures*. Lincoln: University of Nebraska Press, 2006.

The history of national grasslands, a description of the areas that fall into this category, and a discussion of a possible future of these grasslands.

Mutel, Cornelia F. *The Emerald Horizon: The History of Nature in Iowa*. Iowa City: University of Iowa Press, 2008.

An engaging description of prairie as it was, what is left today, and conservation and restoration efforts to replace some of what was lost.

Reichman, O. J. *Konza Prairie: A Tallgrass Natural History*. Lawrence: University Press of Kansas, 1988.

A description of the largest existing remnant of tallgrass prairie, in the Flint Hills of Kansas, including a discussion of its ecology and future.

Savage, Candace. *Prairie: A Natural History*. 2nd ed. Vancouver, BC: Greystone Books, 2011.

A description of the natural history of prairie—plants, animals, and interactions—with photos.

Smith, Daryll, Dave Williams, Greg Houseal, and Kirk Henderson. *The Tallgrass Prairie Center Guide to Prairie Restoration in the Upper Midwest*. Iowa City: University of Iowa Press, 2010.

Another good book for the would-be prairie owner.

Wallace, Marianne D. *America's Prairies and Grasslands: Guide to Plants and Animals.* Golden, CO: Fulcrum, 2001.

This slim book is a perfect introduction to prairie for children.

Winckler, Suzanne *Prairie: A North American Guide.* Iowa City: University of Iowa Press, 2004.

A guide to prairies throughout the central plains region of the United States and Canada.

SOURCES

CHAPTER 1. GLIMPSES OF THE PAST, REALITY OF THE PRESENT

Deliette, Sieur Pierre. *Memoir of De Gannes concerning the Illinois Country.* 1695. Reproduced in translation in Paul M. Angle, ed., *Prairie State: Impressions of Illinois, 1673–1967, by Travelers and Other Observers.* Chicago: University of Chicago Press, 1968, p. 22.

Hall, James. *Notes on the Western States; Containing Descriptive Sketches of Their Soil, Climate, Resources, and Scenery.* Philadelphia: Harrison Hall, 1838, p. 71.

Herre, Albert W. An Early Illinois Prairie. *American Botanist*, vol. 46, 1940, p. 44.

CHAPTER 2. FARMLAND TO PRAIRIE

Mirk, Walter. *An Introduction to the Tallgrass Prairie of the Upper Midwest: Its History, Ecology, Preservation, and Reconstruction.* Boscobel, WI: Prairie Enthusiasts, 1997, p. 60.

CHAPTER 3. FIRE

Blane, William. *An Excursion through the United States and Canada during the Years 1822–23.* London: Baldwin, Cradock, and Joy, 1824, pp. 187–88, 190.

CHAPTER 4. A RAINBOW LANDSCAPE

Steele, Eliza R. *Summer Journey in the West.* New York: John S. Taylor, 1841, p. 126.

CHAPTER 5. SIX LEGS AND EIGHT

Oliver, William. *Eight Months in Illinois, with Information to Immigrants.* 1843. Reprint, Chicago: Walter M. Hill, 1924, p. 148.

CHAPTER 6. FEATHERS AND FUR

Fearon, Henry Bradshaw. *Sketches of America: A Narrative of a Journey of Five Thousand Miles through the Eastern and Western States of America.* 3rd ed. London: Longman, Hurst, Rees, Orme, and Brown, 1819, p. 257.

CHAPTER 7. SEASONS

Farnham, Eliza W. *Life in Prairie Land.* New York: Harper & Brothers, 1846, p. 40.

CHAPTER 8. OPEN SKY

Blane, William. *An Excursion through the United States and Canada during the Years 1822–23.* London: Baldwin, Cradock, and Joy, 1824, p. 184.

Monroe, James. A Letter to Thomas Jefferson, 1786. In *The Writings of James Monroe.* Vol. 1, *1778–1794,* edited by Stanislaus Murray Hamilton. New York: G. P. Putnam's Sons, 1898, p. 117.

Regan, John. *The Western Wilds of America, or, Backwoods and Prairies; and Scenes in the Valley of the Mississippi.* 2nd ed. Edinburgh: John Menzies and W. P. Nimmo, 1859, pp. 46–47.

FRED DELCOMYN, a certified master naturalist and a professor emeritus of the School of Integrative Biology at the University of Illinois, is the author of *Foundations of Neurobiology* and more than 100 popular and scientific articles. Since 2009, he has served on the board of directors of Grand Prairie Friends, an Illinois-based not-for-profit conservation organization and land trust involved with prairie protection and restoration.

JAMES L. ELLIS is the natural areas coordinator for the University of Illinois. A botanist with the Illinois Natural History Survey, he has published articles on prairie ecology, conservation, and management for both academic and general audiences. He has served on the Grand Prairie Friends' board of directors since 2000.

Following page, *we often enjoy an idyllic late-summer day such as this one on the backyard prairie.*